LECTURES AND CONVERSATIONS
ON AESTHETICS, PSYCHOLOGY AND RELIGIOUS BELIEF

L. WITTGENSTEIN

LECTURES & CONVERSATIONS

on *Aesthetics, Psychology and Religious Belief*

Compiled from Notes taken by
Yorick Smythies, Rush Rhees and James Taylor

Edited by Cyril Barrett

BASIL BLACKWELL · OXFORD

FIRST PRINTED 1966
REPRINTED 1967

PRINTED IN GREAT BRITAIN
BY A. T. BROOME AND SON, 18 ST. CLEMENT'S, OXFORD
AND BOUND BY THE KEMP HALL BINDERY, OXFORD

CONTENTS

PREFACE

The first thing to be said about this book is that nothing contained herein was written by Wittgenstein himself. The notes published here are not Wittgenstein's own lecture notes but notes taken down by students, which he neither saw nor checked. It is even doubtful if he would have approved of their publication, at least in their present form. Since, however, they deal with topics only briefly touched upon in his other published writings, and since for some time they have been circulating privately, it was thought best to publish them in a form approved by their authors.

The lectures on aesthetics were delivered in private rooms in Cambridge in the summer of 1938. They were given to a small group of students, which included Rush Rhees, Yorick Smythies, James Taylor, Casmir Lewy, Theodore Redpath and Maurice Drury (whose names occur in the text). The name of another student, Ursell, also occurs in the text (p. 28), but he did not attend the lectures. The lectures on religious belief belong to a course on belief given about the same time. The conversations on Freud between Wittgenstein and Rush Rhees took place between 1942 and 1946.

Besides the notes of the conversations on Freud, those of the fourth lecture on aesthetics are by Rush Rhees; the rest are by Smythies. Since we possess three versions of the first three lectures on aesthetics (by Smythies, Rhees and Taylor—referred to respectively as S, R, and T) and two versions of the fourth lecture, the most complete version has been chosen as the text and significant variants have been added in footnote. The notes have been printed as they were taken down at the time, except for some minor grammatical corrections and a few omissions where the original was indecipherable. Although the different versions agree to a remarkable extent, their authors do not vouch for their accuracy in every detail: they do not claim to give a verbatim report of what Wittgenstein said.

The inclusion of variants may give to what were, after all, no more than informal discussions, an importance and solemnity which may seem inappropriate. On the other hand, as should be clear, the different versions complement and clarify each other, and at the same time hint at their close agreement (which could be demonstrated only by printing all versions in full). It might have been possible to conflate the versions into a single text, but it seemed better to preserve each version as it was taken down and leave the reader to reconstruct a composite text for himself. At times, in the interests of clarity and smoother reading, some of the variants have been introduced into the text. Wherever this is done, and also where editorial emendations have been made, square brackets have been employed. The use of three dots (...) usually indicates that there is a lacuna or an indecipherable passage in the text.

Finally, a word about the choice of material. This is only a selection from the extant students' notes of Wittgenstein's lectures. Yet, in spite of appearances, it is not a random selection. The notes printed here reflect Wittgenstein's opinions on and attitude to life, to religious, psychological and artistic questions. That Wittgenstein himself did not keep these questions separate is clear, for example, from G. E. Moore's account of the 1930–33 lectures (*Mind* 1955).

C. B.

LECTURES ON AESTHETICS

I

1. The subject (Aesthetics) is very big and entirely mis-understood as far as I can see. The use of such a word as 'beautiful' is even more apt to be misunderstood if you look at the linguistic form of sentences in which it occurs than most other words. 'Beautiful' [and 'good'—R] is an adjective, so you are inclined to say: "This has a certain quality, that of being beautiful".

2. We are going from one subject-matter of philosophy to another, from one group of words to another group of words.

3. An intelligent way of dividing up a book on philosophy would be into parts of speech, kinds of words. Where in fact you would have to distinguish far more parts of speech than an ordinary grammar does. You would talk for hours and hours on the verbs 'seeing', 'feeling', etc., verbs describing personal experience. We get a peculiar kind of confusion or confusions which comes up with all these words.[1] You would have another chapter on numerals—here there would be another kind of confusion: a chapter on 'all', 'any', 'some', etc.—another kind of confusion: a chapter on 'you', 'I', etc.—another kind: a chapter on 'beautiful', 'good'—another kind. We get into a new group of confusions; language plays us entirely new tricks.

4. I have often compared language to a tool chest, containing a hammer, chisel, matches, nails, screws, glue. It is not a chance that all these things have been put together—but there are import-ant differences between the different tools—they are used in a family of ways—though nothing could be more different than glue and a chisel. There is constant surprise at the new tricks language plays on us when we get into a new field.

5. One thing we always do when discussing a word is to ask how we were taught it. Doing this on the one hand destroys a variety of misconceptions, on the other hand gives you a primitive language in which the word is used. Although this language is not what you talk when you are twenty, you get a

[1] Here we find similarities—we find peculiar sorts of confusion which come up with *all* these words.—R.

rough approximation to what kind of language game is going to be played. Cf. How did we learn 'I dreamt so and so'? The interesting point is that we didn't learn it by being shown a dream. If you ask yourself how a child learns 'beautiful', 'fine', etc., you find it learns them roughly as interjections. ('Beautiful' is an odd word to talk about because it's hardly ever used.) A child generally applies a word like 'good' first to food. One thing that is immensely important in teaching is exaggerated gestures and facial expressions. The word is taught as a substitute for a facial expression or a gesture. The gestures, tones of voice, etc., in this case are expressions of approval. What *makes* the word an interjection of approval?[1] It is the game it appears in, not the form of words. (If I had to say what is the main mistake made by philosophers of the present generation, including Moore, I would say that it is that when language is looked at, what is looked at is a form of words and not the use made of the form of words.) Language is a characteristic part of a large group of activities—talking, writing, travelling on a bus, meeting a man, etc.[2] We are concentrating, not on the words 'good' or 'beautiful', which are entirely uncharacteristic, generally just subject and predicate ('This is beautiful'), but on the occasions on which they are said—on the enormously complicated situation in which the aesthetic expression has a place, in which the expression itself has almost a negligible place.

6. If you came to a foreign tribe, whose language you didn't know at all and you wished to know what words corresponded to 'good', 'fine', etc., what would you look for? You would look for smiles, gestures, food, toys. ([Reply to objection:] If you went to Mars and men were spheres with sticks coming out, you wouldn't know what to look for. Or if you went to a tribe where noises made with the mouth were just breathing or making music, and language was made with the ears. Cf. "When you see trees swaying about they are talking to one another." ("Every-

[1] And not of disapproval or of surprise, for example?
(The child understands the gestures which you use in teaching him. If he did not, he could understand nothing.)—R.
[2] When we build houses, we talk and write. When I take a bus, I say to the conductor: 'Threepenny.' We are concentrating not just on the word or the sentence in which it is used—which is highly uncharacteristic—but on the occasion on which it is said: the framework in which (nota bene) the actual aesthetic judgment is practically nothing at all.—R.

thing has a soul.") You compare the branches with arms. Certainly we must interpret the gestures of the tribe on the analogy of ours.) How far this takes us from normal aesthetics [and ethics—T]. We don't start from certain words, but from certain occasions or activities.

7. A characteristic thing about our language is that a large number of words used under these circumstances are adjectives —'fine', 'lovely', etc. But you see that this is by no means necessary. You saw that they were first used as interjections. Would it matter if instead of saying "This is lovely", I just said "Ah!" and smiled, or just rubbed my stomach? As far as these primitive languages go, problems about what these words are about, what their real subject is, [which is called 'beautiful' or 'good'.—R.][1] don't come up at all.

8. It is remarkable that in real life, when aesthetic judgements are made, aesthetic adjectives such as 'beautiful', 'fine', etc., play hardly any role at all. Are aesthetic adjectives used in a musical criticism? You say: "Look at this transition",[2] or [Rhees] "The passage here is incoherent". Or you say, in a poetical criticism, [Taylor]: "His use of images is precise". The words you use are more akin to 'right' and 'correct' (as these words are used in ordinary speech) than to 'beautiful' and 'lovely'.[3]

9. Words such as 'lovely' are first used as interjections. Later they are used on very few occasions. We might say of a piece of music that it is lovely, by this not praising it but giving it a character. (A lot of people, of course, who can't express themselves properly use the word very frequently. As they use it, it is used as an interjection.) I might ask: "For what melody would I most like to use the word 'lovely'?" I might choose between calling a melody 'lovely' and calling it 'youthful'. It is stupid to call a piece of music 'Spring Melody' or 'Spring Symphony'. But the word 'springy' wouldn't be absurd at all, any more than 'stately' or 'pompous'.

[1] What the thing that is really good is—T.
[2] 'The transition was made in the right way.'—T.
[3] It would be better to use 'lovely' descriptively, on a level with 'stately', 'pompous,' etc.—T.

10. If I were a good draughtsman, I could convey an innumerable number of expressions by four strokes—

Such words as 'pompous' and 'stately' could be expressed by faces. Doing this, our descriptions would be much more flexible and various than they are as expressed by adjectives. If I say of a piece of Schubert's that it is melancholy, that is like giving it a face (I don't express approval or disapproval). I could instead use gestures or [Rhees] dancing. In fact, if we want to be exact, we do use a gesture or a facial expression.

11. [*Rhees*: What rule are we using or referring to when we say: "This is the correct way"? If a music teacher says a piece *should* be played this way and plays it, what is he appealing to?]

12. Take the question: "How should poetry be read? What is the correct way of reading it?" If you are talking about blank verse the right way of reading it might be stressing it correctly— you discuss how far you should stress the rhythm and how far you should hide it. A man says it ought to be read *this* way and reads it out to you. You say: "Oh yes. Now it makes sense." There are cases of poetry which should almost be scanned— where the metre is as clear as crystal—others where the metre is entirely in the background. I had an experience with the 18th century poet Klopstock.[1] I found that the way to read him was to stress his metre abnormally. Klopstock put ◡—◡ (etc.) in front of his poems. When I read his poems in this new way, I said: "Ah-ha, now I know why he did this." What had happened? I had read this kind of stuff and had been moderately bored, but when I read it in this particular way, intensely, I smiled, said: "This is *grand*," etc. But I might not have said anything. The important fact was that I read it again and again. When I read these poems I made gestures and facial expressions which were what would be called gestures of approval. But the important

[1] Friedrich Gottlieb Klopstock (1724–1803). Wittgenstein is referring to the Odes. (*Gesammelte Werke*, Stuttgart, 1886–7). Klopstock believed that poetic diction was distinct from popular language. He rejected rhyme as vulgar and introduced instead the metres of ancient literature.—Ed.

thing was that I read the poems entirely differently, more intensely, and said to others: "Look! This is how they should be read."[1] Aesthetic adjectives played hardly any role.

13. What does a person who knows a good suit say when trying on a suit at the tailor's? "That's the right length", "That's too short", "That's too narrow". Words of approval play no rôle, although he will look pleased when the coat suits him. Instead of "That's too short" I might say "Look!" or instead of "Right" I might say "Leave it as it is". A good cutter may not use any words at all, but just make a chalk mark and later alter it. How do I show my approval of a suit? Chiefly by wearing it often, liking it when it is seen, etc.

14. (If I give you the light and shadow on a body in a picture I can thereby give you the shape of it. But if I give you the highlights in a picture you don't know what the shape is.)

15. In the case of the word 'correct' you have a variety of related cases. There is first the case in which you learn the rules. The cutter learns how long a coat is to be, how wide the sleeve must be, etc. He learns rules—he is drilled—as in music you are drilled in harmony and counterpoint. Suppose I went in for tailoring and I first learnt all the rules, I might have, on the whole, two sorts of attitude. (1) Lewy says: "This is too short." I say: "No. It is right. It is according to the rules." (2) I develop a feeling for the rules. I interpret the rules. I might say: "No. It isn't right. It isn't according to the rules."[2] Here I would be making an aesthetic judgement about the thing which is according to the rules in sense (1). On the other hand, if I hadn't learnt the rules, I wouldn't be able to make the aesthetic judgement. In learning the rules you get a more and more refined judgement. Learning the rules actually changes your judgement. (Although, if you haven't learnt Harmony and haven't a good ear, you may nevertheless detect any disharmony in a sequence of chords.)

16. You could regard the rules laid down for the measurement of a coat as an expression of what certain people want.[3] People separated on the point of what a coat should measure:

[1] If we speak of the right way to read a piece of poetry—approval enters, but it plays a fairly small role in the situation.—R.
[2] 'Don't you see that if we made it broader, it isn't right and it isn't according to the rules.'—R.
[3] These may be extremely explicit and taught, or not formulated at all.—T.

there were some who didn't care if it was broad or narrow, etc.; there were others who cared an enormous lot.[1] The rules of harmony, you can say, expressed the way people wanted chords to follow—their wishes crystallized in these rules (the word 'wishes' is much too vague.)[2] All the greatest composers wrote in accordance with them. ([Reply to objection:] You can say that every composer changed the rules, but the variation was very slight; not all the rules were changed. The music was still good by a great many of the old rules.—This though shouldn't come in here.)

17.   In what we call the Arts a person who has judgement develops. (A person who has a judgement doesn't mean a person who says 'Marvellous!' at certain things.)[3] If we talk of aesthetic judgements, we think, among a thousand things, of the Arts. When we make an aesthetic judgement about a thing, we do not just gape at it and say: "Oh! How marvellous!" We distinguish between a person who knows what he is talking about and a person who doesn't.[4] If a person is to admire English poetry, he must know English. Suppose that a Russian who doesn't know English is overwhelmed by a sonnet admitted to be good. We would say that he does not know what is in it at all. Similarly, of a person who doesn't know metres but who is overwhelmed, we would say that he doesn't know what's in it. In music this is more pronounced. Suppose there is a person who admires and enjoys what is admitted to be good but can't remember the simplest tunes, doesn't know when the bass comes in, etc. We say he hasn't seen what's in it. We use the phrase 'A man is musical' not so as to call a man musical if he says "Ah!" when a piece of music is played, any more than we call a dog musical if it wags its tail when music is played.[5]

[1] But—it is just a fact that people have laid down such and such rules. We say 'people' but in fact it was a particular class. . . . When we say 'people', these were *some* people.—R.

[2] And although we have talked of 'wishes' here, the fact is just that these rules were laid down.—R.

[3] In what we call the arts there developed what we call a 'judge'—i.e. one who has judgement. This does not mean just someone who admires or does not admire. We have an entirely new element.—R.

[4] He must react in a consistent way over a long period. Must know all sorts of things.—T.

[5] Cf. the person who likes hearing music but cannot talk about it at all, and is quite unintelligent on the subject. 'He is musical'. We do not say this if he is just happy when he hears music and the other things aren't present.—T.

18. The word we ought to talk about is 'appreciated'. What does appreciation consist in ?

19. If a man goes through an endless number of patterns in a tailor's, [and] says: "No. This is slightly too dark. This is slightly too loud", etc., he is what we call an appreciator of material. That he is an appreciator is not shown by the interjections he uses, but by the way he chooses, selects, etc. Similarly in music: "Does this harmonize? No. The bass is not quite loud enough. Here I just want something different. . . ." This is what we call an appreciation.

20. It is not only difficult to describe what appreciation consists in, but impossible. To describe what it consists in we would have to describe the whole environment.

21. I know exactly what happens when a person who knows a lot about suits goes to the tailor, also I know what happens when a person who knows nothing about suits goes—what he says, how he acts, etc.[1] There is an extraordinary number of different cases of appreciation. And, of course, what I know is nothing compared to what one could know. I would have—to say what appreciation is—e.g. to explain such an enormous wart as arts and crafts, such a particular kind of disease. Also I would have to explain what our photographers do today—and why it is impossible to get a decent picture of your friend even if you pay £1,000.

22. You can get a picture of what you may call a very high culture, e.g. German music in the last century and the century before, and what happens when this deteriorates. A picture of what happens in Architecture when you get imitations—or when thousands of people are interested in the minutest details. A picture of what happens when a dining-room table is chosen more or less at random, when no one knows where it came from.[2]

23. We talked of correctness. A good cutter won't use any words except words like 'Too long', 'All right'. When we talk of

[1] That is aesthetics.—T.

[2] Explain what happens when a craft deteriorates. A period in which everything is fixed and extraordinary care is lavished on certain details; and a period in which everything is copied and nothing is thought about.—T.

A great number of people are highly interested in a detail of a dining-room chair. And then there is a period when a dining-room chair is in the drawing-room and no one knows where this came from or that people had once given enormous thought in order to know how to design it.—R.

a Symphony of Beethoven we don't talk of correctness. Entirely different things enter. One wouldn't talk of appreciating the *tremendous* things in Art. In certain styles in Architecture a door is correct, and the thing is you appreciate it. But in the case of a Gothic Cathedral what we do is not at all to find it correct—it plays an entirely different role with us.[1] The entire *game* is different. It is as different as to judge a human being and on the one hand to say 'He behaves well' and on the other hand 'He made a great impression on me'.

24. 'Correctly', 'charmingly', 'finely', etc. play an entirely different role. Cf. the famous address of Buffon—a terrific man —on style in writing; making ever so many distinctions which I only understand vaguely but which he didn't mean vaguely—all kinds of nuances like 'grand', 'charming', 'nice'.[2]

25. The words we call expressions of aesthetic judgement play a very complicated role, but a very definite role, in what we call a culture of a period. To describe their use or to describe what you mean by a cultured taste, you have to describe a culture.[3] What we now call a cultured taste perhaps didn't exist in the Middle Ages. An entirely different game is played in different ages.

26. What belongs to a language game is a whole culture. In describing musical taste you have to describe whether children give concerts, whether women do or whether men only give them, etc., etc.[4] In aristocratic circles in Vienna people had [such and such] a taste, then it came into bourgeois circles and women joined choirs, etc. This is an example of tradition in music.

27. [*Rhees*: Is there tradition in Negro art? Could a European appreciate Negro art?]

28. What would tradition in Negro Art be? That women wear cut-grass skirts? etc., etc. I don't know. I don't know how Frank Dobson's appreciation of Negro Art compares with an

---

[1] Here there is no question of *degree.*—R.

[2] *Discours sur le style*: the address on his reception into L'Academie Française. 1753.—Ed.

[3] To describe a set ot aesthetic rules fully means really to describe the culture of a period.—T.

[4] That children are taught by adults who go to concerts, etc., that the schools are like they are, etc.—R.

educated Negro's.[1] If you say he appreciates it, I don't yet know what this means.[2] He may fill his room with objects of Negro Art. Does he just say: "Ah!"? Or does he do what the best-Negro musicians do? Or does he agree or disagree with so and so about it? You may call this appreciation. Entirely different to an educated Negro's. Though an educated Negro may also have Negro objects of art in his room. The Negro's and Frank Dobson's are different appreciations altogether. You do something different with them. Suppose Negroes dress in their own way and I say I appreciate a good Negro tunic—does this mean I would have one made, or that I would say (as at the tailor's): "No...this is too long", or does it mean I say: "How charming!"?

29. Suppose Lewy has what is called a cultured taste in painting. This is something entirely different to what was called a cultured taste in the fifteenth century. An entirely different game was played. He does something entirely different with it to what a man did then.

30. There are lots of people, well-offish, who have been to good schools, who can afford to travel about and see the Louvre, etc., and who know a lot about and can talk fluently about dozens of painters. There is another person who has seen very few paintings, but who looks intensely at one or two paintings which make a profound impression on him.[3] Another person who is broad, neither deep nor wide. Another person who is very narrow, concentrated and circumscribed. Are these different kinds of appreciation? They may all be called 'appreciation'.

31. You talk in entirely different terms of the Coronation robe of Edward II and of a dress suit.[4] What did *they* do and say about Coronation robes? Was the Coronation robe made by a tailor? Perhaps it was designed by Italian artists who had their own traditions; never seen by Edward II until he put it on. Questions like 'What standards were there?', etc. are all relevant

---

[1] Frank Dobson (1888–1963) painter and sculptor; was the first to bring to England the interest in African and Asian sculpture which characterized the work of Picasso and the other Cubists during the years immediately preceeding and following the First World War.—Ed.

[2] Here you haven't made what you mean by 'appreciate Negro Art' clear.—T.

[3] Someone who has not travelled but who makes certain observations which show that he 'really does appreciate' ... an appreciation which concentrates on one thing and is very deep—so that you would give your last penny for it.—R.

[4] Edward the Confessor.—T.

B

to the question 'Could you criticize the robe as they critized it?'. You appreciate it in an entirely different way; your attitude to it is entirely different to that of a person living at the time it was designed. On the other hand 'This is a fine Coronation robe!' might have been said by a man at the time in exactly the same way as a man says it now.

32.   I draw your attention to differences and say: "Look how different these differences are!" "Look what is in common to the different cases", "Look what is common to Aesthetic judgements". An immensely complicated family of cases is left, with the highlight—the expression of admiration, a smile or a gesture, etc.

33.   [Rhees asked Wittgenstein some question about his 'theory' of deterioration.]

Do you think I have a theory? Do you think I'm saying what deterioration is? What I do is describe different things called deterioration. I might approve deterioration—"All very well your fine musical culture; I'm very glad children don't learn harmony now." [Rhees: Doesn't what you say imply a preference for using 'deterioration' in certain ways?] All right, if you like, but this by the way—no, it is no matter. My example of deterioration is an example of something I know, perhaps something I dislike—I don't know. 'Deterioration' applies to a tiny bit I may know.

34.   Our dress is in a way simpler than dress in the 18th century and more a dress adapted to certain violent activities, such as bicycling, walking, etc. Suppose we notice a similar change in Architecture and in hairdressing, etc. Suppose I talked of the deterioration of the style of living.[1] If someone asks: "What do you mean by deterioration?" I describe, give examples. You use 'deterioration' on the one hand to describe a particular kind of development, on the other hand to express disapproval. I may join it up with the things I like; you with the things you dislike. But the word may be used without any affective element; you use it to describe a particular kind of thing that happened.[2] It was more like using a technical term—possibly,

---

[1] Deterioration of style and of living.—R.
[2] 'Deterioration' gets its sense from the examples I can give. 'That's a deterioration,' may be an expression of disapproval or a description.

though not at all necessarily, with a derogatory element in it. You may say in protest, when I talk of deterioration: "But this was very good." I say: "All right. But this wasn't what I was talking about. I used it to describe a particular kind of development."

35.   In order to get clear about aesthetic words you have to describe ways of living.[1] We think we have to talk about aesthetic judgements like 'This is beautiful', but we find that if we have to talk about aesthetic judgements we don't find these words at all, but a word used something like a gesture, accompanying a complicated activity.[2]

36.   [*Lewy*: If my landlady says a picture is lovely and I say it is hideous, we don't contradict one another.]

In a sense [and in *certain examples*—R] you do contradict one another. She dusts it carefully, looks at it often, etc. You want to throw it in the fire. This is just the stupid kind of example which is given in philosophy, as if things like 'This is hideous', 'This is lovely' were the only kinds of things ever said. But it is only one thing amongst a vast realm of other things—one special case. Suppose the landlady says: "This is hideous", and you say: "This is lovely"—all right, that's that.

II

1.   One interesting thing is the idea that people have of a kind of science of Aesthetics. I would almost like to talk of what could be meant by Aesthetics.

2.   You might think Aesthetics is a science telling us what's beautiful—almost too ridiculous for words. I suppose it ought to include also what sort of coffee tastes well.[3]

3.   I see roughly this—there is a realm of utterance of delight, when you taste pleasant food or smell a pleasant smell, etc., then there is the realm of Art which is quite different, though often you

---

[1] Cf. 'This is a fine dress.'—R.

[2] The judgment is a gesture accompanying a vast structure of actions not expressed by one judgment.—R.

'This is fine' is on a level with a gesture, almost—connected with all sorts of other gestures and actions and a whole situation and a culture. In Aesthetics just as in the arts what we called expletives play a very small part. The adjectives used in these are closer related to 'correct'.—T.

[3] It is hard to find boundaries.—R.

may make the same face when you hear a piece of music as when you taste good food. (Though you may cry at something you like very much.)

4. Supposing you meet someone in the street and he tells you he has lost his greatest friend, in a voice extremely expressive of his emotion.[1] You might say: "It was extraordinarily beautiful, the way he expressed himself." Supposing you then asked: "What similarity has my admiring this person with my eating vanilla ice and liking it?" To compare them seems almost disgusting. (But you can connect them by intermediate cases.) Suppose someone said: "But this is a quite different kind of delight." But did you learn two meanings of 'delight'? You use the same word on both occasions.[2] There is some connection between these delights. Although in the first case the emotion of delight would in our judgement hardly count.[3]

5. It is like saying: "I classify works of Art in this way: at some I look up and at some I look down." This way of classifying might be interesting.[4] We might discover all sorts of connections between looking up or down at works of Art and looking up or down at other things. If we found, perhaps, that eating vanilla ice made us look up, we might not attach great importance to looking up. There may be a realm, a small realm of experiences which may make me look up or down where I can infer a lot from the fact that I looked up or down; another realm of experiences where nothing can be inferred from my looking up or down.[5] Cf wearing blue or green trousers may in a certain society mean a lot, but in another society it may not mean anything.

6. What are expressions of liking something? Is it only what we say or interjections we use or faces we make? Obviously not. It is, often, how often I read something or how often I wear a suit. Perhaps I won't even say: "It's fine", but wear it often and look at it.[6]

[1] Someone . . . who tells you he has lost his friend, in a restrained way.—R.
[2] But notice that you use the same word and not in the same chance way you use the same word 'bank' for two things [like 'river bank' and 'money bank'—R.] —T.
[3] Although in the first case the gesture or expression of delight may be most unimportant in a way.—T.
[4] You might discover further characters of things which make us look up—.R.
[5] Some one might exaggerate the importance of the type of indication.—T.
[6] If I like a suit I may buy it, or wear it often—without interjections or making faces.—R. I may never smile at it.—T.

7. Suppose we build houses and we give doors and windows certain dimensions. Does the fact that we *like* these dimensions necessarily show in anything we say? Is what we like necessarily shown by an expression of *liking*?[1] [For instance—R] suppose our children draw windows and when they draw them in the wrong way we punish them. Or when someone builds a certain house we refuse to live in it or run away.

8. Take the case of fashions. How does a fashion come about? Say, we wear lapels broader than last year. Does this mean that the tailors like them better broader? No, not necessarily. He cuts it like this and this year he makes it broader. Perhaps this year he finds it too narrow and makes it wider. Perhaps no expression [of delight—R] is used at all.[2]

9. You design a door and look at it and say: "Higher, higher, higher . . . oh, all right."[3] (Gesture) What is this? Is it an expression of content?

10. Perhaps the most important thing in connection with aesthetics is what may be called aesthetic reactions, e.g. discontent, disgust, discomfort. The expression of discontent is not the same as the expression of discomfort. The expression of discontent says: "Make it higher . . . too low! . . . do something to this."

11. Is what I call an expression of discontent something like an expression of discomfort *plus* knowing the cause of the discomfort and asking for it to be removed? If I say: "This door is too low. Make it higher", should we say I know the cause of my discomfort?

12. 'Cause' is used in very many different ways, e.g.

(1) "What is the cause of unemployment?" "What is the cause of this expression?"

(2) "What was the cause of your jumping?" "That noise."

(3) "What was the cause of that wheel going round?" You trace a mechanism.[4]

---

[1] Our preferring these shows itself in all sorts of ways.—T.
[2] But the tailor does not say: 'This is nice.' He is a good cutter. He is just contented.—R. If you mean 'this year he cuts it broader' then you can say this. This way we are contented, the other not.—T.
[3] '. . . *there*: thank God.'—R. '. . . yes, that's right.'—T.
[4] Cause: (1) Experiment and statistics.
　　　(2) Reason.
　　　(3) Mechanism.—T.

13. [*Redpath*: "Making the door higher removes your discontent."]

Wittgenstein asked: "Why is this a bad way of putting it?" It is in the wrong form because it presupposes '—removes—'.

14. Saying you know the cause of your discomfort could mean two things.

(1) I predict correctly that if you lower the door, I will be satisfied.

(2) But that when in fact I say: "Too high!" 'Too high!' is in this case not conjecture. Is 'Too high' comparable with 'I think I had too many tomatoes today'?

15. If I ask: "If I make it lower will your discomfort cease?", you may say: "I'm *sure* it will." The important thing is that I say: "Too high!" It is a reaction analogous to my taking my hand away from a hot plate—which may not relieve my discomfort. The reaction peculiar to this discomfort is saying 'Too high' or whatever it is.

16. To say: "I feel discomfort and know the cause", is entirely misleading because 'know the cause' normally means something quite different. How misleading it is depends on whether when you said: "I know the cause", you meant it to be an explanation or not. 'I feel discomfort and know the cause' makes it sound as if there were two things going on in my soul—discomfort and knowing the cause.

17. In these cases the word 'cause' is hardly ever used at all. You use 'why?' and 'because', but not 'cause'.[1]

18. We have here a kind of discomfort which you may call 'directed', e.g. if I am afraid of you, my discomfort is directed.[2] Saying 'I know the cause' brings in mind the case of statistics or tracing a mechanism. If I say: "I know the cause", it looks as if I had analysed the feelings (as I analyse the feeling of hearing my own voice and, at the same time, rubbing my hands) which, of course, I haven't done. We have given, as it were, a *grammatical* explanation [in saying, the feeling is 'directed'].

19. There is a 'Why?' to aesthetic discomfort not a 'cause' to it. The expression of discomfort takes the form of a criticism

---

[1] Why are you disgusted? Because it is too high.—R.

[2] What is the advantage of 'My feeling of fear is directed' as opposed to 'I know the cause'?—R.

and not 'My mind is not at rest' or something. It might take the form of looking at a picture and saying: "What's wrong with it?"[1]

20. It's all very well to say: "Can't we get rid of this analogy?" Well, we cannot. If we think of discomfort—cause, pain—cause of pain naturally suggests itself.

21. The cause, in the sense of the object it is directed to is also the cause in other senses. When you remove it, the discomfort ceases and what not.

22. If one says: "Can we be immediately aware of the cause?", the first thing that comes into our mind is not statistics [(as in 'the cause of the rise in unemployment')—R], but tracing a mechanism. It has so very often been said that if something has been caused by something else this is only a matter of concomitance. Isn't this very queer? Very queer. 'It's only concomitance' shows you think it can be something else.[2] It could be an experiential proposition, but then I don't know what it would be. Saying this shows you know of something different, i.e. connection. What are they denying when they say: "There is no necessary connection"?

23. You say constantly in philosophy things like: "People say there is a super-mechanism, but there isn't." But no one knows what a super-mechanism is.

24. (The idea of a super-mechanism doesn't really come in here. What comes in is the idea of a mechanism.)

25. We have the idea of a super-mechanism when we talk of logical necessity, e.g. physics tried as an ideal to reduce things to mechanisms or something hitting something else.[3]

26. We say that people condemn a man to death and then we say the Law condemns him to death. "Although the Jury can

[1] If I look at a picture and say: 'What's wrong with this?', then it is better to say that my feeling has direction, and not that my feeling has a cause and I don't know what it is. Otherwise we suggest an analogy with 'pain' and 'cause of pain'—i.e. what you have eaten. This is wrong or misleading, because, although we do use the word 'cause' in the sense of 'what it is directed to' ('What made you jump?'—'Seeing him appear in the doorway'), we often use it in other senses also.—R.

[2] If you say: 'To speak of the cause of some development is only to speak of the concomitants'—'cause is only a question of concomitants'—then if you put 'only', you are admitting that it could be something else. It means that you know of something entirely different.—R.

[3] You want to say: 'Surely there is a connection.' But what is a connection? Well, levers, chains, cogwheels. These are connections, and here we have them. but here what we ought to explain is 'super'.—R.

pardon [acquit?] him, the Law can't." (This *may* mean the Law can't take bribes, etc.) The idea of something super-strict, something stricter than any Judge can be,[1] super-rigidity. The point being, you are inclined to ask: "Do we have a picture of something more rigorous?" Hardly. But we are inclined to express ourselves in the form of a superlative.

27.

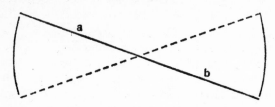

Cf. a lever-fulcrum. The idea of a super-hardness. "The geometrical lever is harder than any lever can be. It can't bend." Here you have the case of logical necessity. "Logic is a mechanism made of an infinitely hard material. Logic cannot bend.'[2] (Well, no more it can.) This is the way we arrive at a super-something. This is the way certain superlatives come about, how they are used, e.g. the infinite.

28. People would say that even in the case of tracing a mechanism there is also concomitance. But need there be? I just follow the string to the person at the other end.

29. Suppose there was a super-mechanism in the sense that there was a mechanism inside the string. Even if there was such a mechanism, it would do no good. You do recognize tracing the mechanism as tracing a peculiar kind of causal reaction.

30. You wish to get rid of the idea of connection altogether. "This is also only concomitance." Then there is nothing more to be said.[3] You would have to specify what is a case you wouldn't

[1] Something that cannot be swayed.—R.

[2] Suppose that we treat of kinematics. Give the distance of the lever from the point, and calculate the distance of the arc.

But then we say: 'If the lever is made of metal, however hard, it will bend a little, and the point will not come just there.' And so we have the idea of a super-rigidity: the idea of a *geometrical* lever which *cannot* bend. Here we have the idea of logical necessity: a mechanism of infinitely hard material.—R.

If someone says: 'You mustn't think that logic is made of an infinitely hard material', you must ask: 'What mustn't I think?'—T.

[3] What we call *'explanation'* is a form of *connection*. And we wish to get rid of connection altogether. We wish to get rid of the notion of mechanism, and say: 'It's all concomitants.' Why 'all'?—R.

call concomitance. "Tracing a mechanism is only finding concomitance. In the end it can all be reduced to concomitance." It might be proved that people never traced a mechanism unless they had had a lot of experience of a certain sort. This could be put in the way: "It all reduces to concomitance."

31. Cf. "Physics doesn't explain anything. It just describes cases of concomitance."

32. You could mean by 'There is no super-mechanism', 'Don't imagine mechanisms between the atoms in the case of a lever. There aren't any mechanisms there'.[1] (You are taking for granted the atomistic picture.[2] What does this come to? We are so used to this picture that it's as though we had all seen atoms. Every educated eight-year old child knows that things are made of atoms. We would think it lack of education if a person didn't think of a rod as being made of atoms.)

33. (You can look on the mechanism as a set of concomitant causal phenomena. You don't, of course.) You say: "Well, this moves this, this this, this this, and so on."

34. Tracing a mechanism is one way of finding the cause; we speak of 'the cause' in this case. But if cases of wheels made of butter and looking like steel were frequent we might say: "This ('this wheel') is not the only cause at all. This may only look like a mechanism."[3]

35. People often say that aesthetics is a branch of psychology. The idea is that once we are more advanced, everything—all the mysteries of Art—will be understood by psychological experiments. Exceedingly stupid as the idea is, this is roughly it.

36. Aesthetic questions have nothing to do with psychological experiments, but are answered in an entirely different way.[4]

---

[1] You reduce the actual mechanism to a more complicated atomicmechanis m, but don't go on.—T.

[2] We might have a primitive mechanism. Then we have the picture of its all being formed of particles—atoms, etc. And we might then want to say: 'Don't go on to think of atoms between these atoms.' Here we take for granted the atomic picture—which is a queer business. If we had to say what a super-mechanism was, we might say it was one which did not consist of atoms: bits of the mechanism were just solid.—R.

[3] We are constantly inclined to reduce things to other things. So excited by finding that it's sometimes concomitance, we wish to say it's all *really* concomitance. —T.

[4] I wish to make it clear that the important problems in aesthetics are not settled by psychological research.—T.

These problems are answered in a different way—more in the form 'What is in my mind when I say so and so?'—R.

37. "What is in my mind when I say so and so?"[1] I write a sentence. One word isn't the one I need. I find the right word. "What is it I want to say? Oh yes, that is what I wanted." The answer in these cases is the one that satisfied you, e.g. someone says (as we often say in philosophy): "I will tell you what is at the back of your mind: . . ."

"Oh yes, quite so."

The criterion for it being the one that was in your mind is that when I tell you, you agree. This is not what is called a psychological experiment. An example of a psychological experiment is: you have twelve subjects, put same question to each and the result is that each says such and such, i.e. the result is something statistical.[2]

38. You could say: "An aesthetic explanation is not a causal explanation."[3]

39. Cf. Freud: *Wit and the Unconscious*. Freud wrote about jokes. You might call the explanation Freud gives a causal explanation. "If it is not causal, how do you know it's correct?" You say: "Yes, that's right."[4] Freud transforms the joke into a different form which is recognized by us as an expression of the chain of ideas which led us from one end to another of a joke. An entirely new account of a correct explanation. Not one agreeing with experience, but one accepted. You have to give the explanation that is accepted. This is the whole point of the explanation.

40. Cf. "Why do I say "Higher!"?" with "Why do I say "I have a pain"?"[5]

---

[1] Compare: 'What people really want to say is so and so.'—R.

[2] Is this a narrowing of the sense of psychological experiment?—T.

[3] It is true that 'psychology' is used in very different ways. We could say that aesthetic explanation is not causal explanation. Or that it is causal explanation of this sort: that the person who agrees with you sees the cause at once.—R.

[4] All we can say is that if it is presented to you, you say 'Yes, that's what happened.'—R.

[5] The unrest when you ask: 'Why?' in this sort of case is similar to the unrest in the case of 'Why?' when you look for the mechanism. 'Explanation' here is on the level of utterance. In some respect on a level. Cf. the two games with 'He's in pain.' Cf the two games with 'He's in pain.'—T.

Here 'explanation' is on the same level as an utterance—where the utterance (when you say that you have pain, for instance) is the sole criterion. Explanation here is like an utterance supplied by another person—like teaching him to cry. (This takes the surprisingness away from the fact that the whole point of an explanation is that it is accepted. There are corresponding to these explanations utterances which look like this; just as there are utterances which look like assertions.)—R.

III

1.   One asks such a question as 'What does this remind me of?"
or one says of a piece of music: "This is like some sentence, but
what sentence is it like?"[1] Various things are suggested; one
thing, as you say, clicks. What does it mean, it 'clicks'? Does it
do anything you can compare to the noise of a click? Is there the
ringing of a bell, or something comparable?[2]

2.   It is as though you needed some criterion, namely the
clicking, to know the right thing has happened.[3]

3.   The comparison is, that some one particular phenomenon
happened other than my saying: "That's right." You say: "That
explanation is the right one which clicks." Suppose someone
said: "The tempo of that song will be all right when I can hear
distinctly such and such."[4] I have pointed to a phenomenon
which, if it is the case, will make me satisfied.

4.   You might say the clicking is that I'm satisfied. Take a
pointer moving into place opposite another one. You are satisfied
when the two pointers are opposite one another.[5] And you could
have said this in advance.[6]

5.   We are again and again using this simile of something
clicking or fitting, when really there is nothing that clicks or
that fits anything.

6.   I should like to talk of the sort of explanation one longs
for when one talks about an aesthetic impression.

7.   People still have the idea that psychology is one day
going to explain all our aesthetic judgements, and they mean
experimental psychology. This is very funny—very funny
indeed. There doesn't seem any connection between what
psychologists do and any judgement about a work of art. We

[1] There may be an 'explanation' in the form of an answer to a question like 'What does this remind me of?'. In a piece of music there may be a theme of which I say. . .—R.

[2] Does it click in any sense? So that, for instance, you say: 'Now it has made that noise'? Of course not. What do we compare the clicking with here? 'With a feeling,' 'So you have a feeling?' Do you have a sign that it has fallen into place? —R.

[3] Is there any necessary criterion for this happening?—T.

[4] If it is sung slowly. . .—R. played by degrees faster. . .—T.

[5] (Something moving along a circumference, clicks when it falls into place.) —T.

[6] But why not say the clicking is just that I am satisfied? Whereas it might look as though clicking were something else, which I wait for, and when it comes I am satisfied. In some circumstances you *could* point to such a phenomenon.—R.

might examine what sort of thing we would call an explanation of an aesthetic judgement.

8.   Supposing it was found that all our judgements proceeded from our brain. We discovered particular kinds of mechanism in the brain, formulated general laws, etc. One could show that this sequence of notes produces this particular kind of reaction; makes a man smile and say: "Oh, how wonderful."[1] (Mechanism for English language, etc.)[2] Suppose this were done, it might enable us to predict what a particular person would like and dislike. We could calculate these things. The question is whether this is the sort of explanation we should like to have when we are puzzled about aesthetic impressions, e.g. there is a puzzle—"Why do these bars give me such a peculiar impression?" Obviously it isn't this, i.e. a calculation, an account of reactions, etc., we want—apart from the obvious impossibility of the thing.

9.   As far as one can see the puzzlement I am talking about can be cured only by peculiar kinds of comparisons, e.g. by an arrangement of certain musical figures, comparing their effect on us.[3] "If we put in this chord it does not have that effect; if we put in this chord it does." You could have a sentence and say "This sentence sounds queer somehow". You could point what's queer. What would be the criterion that you had pointed out the right thing? Suppose a poem sounded old-fashioned, what would be the criterion that you had found out what was old-fashioned in it? One criterion would be that when something was pointed out you were satisfied. And another criterion: "No-one would use that word today"[4]; here you might refer to a dictionary, ask other people, etc.[5] I *could* point out the wrong thing and yet you would still be satisfied.

10.   Suppose someone heard syncopated music of Brahms played and asked: "What is the queer rhythm which makes me wobble?"[6] "It is the 3 against 4." One could play certain phrases

---

[1] If you knew the mechanism of molecules there, and then knew the sequence of notes in the music, we could show that. . .—R.

[2] That he says it in English and not in French would also be explained by the fact that something is embodied in his brain: we could see the differences.—R.

[3] When the written notes or the played notes are spread out, then you say. . .T.

[4] 'It is this word, you see. No one today would say so and so.'—R.

[5] Suppose you asked: 'What is it that sounds American about this sentence?' But you could find out whether the word was an americanism or not, for instance; other people might corroborate this.—R.

[6] Feel wobbly.—R.

and he would say: "Yes. It's this peculiar rhythm I meant." On the other hand, if he didn't agree, this wouldn't be the explanation.

11.   The sort of explanation one is looking for when one is puzzled by an aesthetic impression is not a causal explanation, not one corroborated by experience or by statistics as to how people react.[1] One of the curious [characteristic—R] things about psychological experiments is that they have to be made on a number of subjects. It is the agreements of Smith, Jones and Robinson which allows you to give an explanation—in this sense of explanation, e.g. you can try out a piece of music in a psychological laboratory and get the result that the music acts in such and such a way under such and such a drug.[2] This is not what one means or what one is driving at by an investigation into aesthetics.

12.   This is connected with the difference between cause and motive. In a law-court you are asked the motive of your action and you are supposed to know it. Unless you lie you are supposed to be able to tell the motive of your action. You are not supposed to know the laws by which your body and mind are governed. Why do they suppose you know it? Because you've had such a lot of experience with yourself? People sometimes say: "No-one can see inside you, but you can see inside yourself", as though being so near yourself, being yourself, you know your own mechanism.[3] But is it like that? "Surely he must know why he did it or why he said such and such."

13.   One case is, where you give the reason for your doing something.[4] "Why did you write 6249 under the line?" You give the multiplication you had done. "I arrived at it by this multiplication." This is comparable to giving a mechanism. One might call it giving a motive for writing down the numbers. It means, I passed through such and such a process of reasoning.[5]

---

[1] You cannot arrive at the explanation by means of psychological experiment.—R.

[2] Or on people of a certain race.—R.

[3] Obviously this has nothing to do with your having observed yourself so often. (Often we do seem to suggest that because you are so near to yourself, you could see what happened. This is like knowing your own mechanism.)—R.

[4] There is one thing here that could be compared with knowing a mechanism—'Surely he must know why he did it, or why he said so and so.' But how do you know why you did it? There is one kind of case where the answer is to give the *reason*: you are writing out a multiplication, and I ask. . .—R.

[5] Where I give a reason in this sense. . .—R.

Here 'Why did you do it?' means 'How did you get there?'. You give a reason, the road you went.

14.   If he tells us a peculiar process by which he arrived at the thing, this inclines us to say: "Only he knows the process which led to it."

15.   Giving a reason sometimes means 'I actually went this way', sometimes 'I could have gone this way', i.e. sometimes what we say acts as a justification, not as a report of what was done, e.g. I *remember* the answer to a question; when asked why I give this answer, I gave a process leading to it, though I didn't go through this process.[1]

16.   "Why did you do it?"   Answer: "I said to myself such and such . . ."   In many cases the motive is just what we give on being asked.[2]

17.   When you ask: "Why did you do it?", in an enormous number of cases people give an answer—apodictic—and are unshakable about it, and in an enormous number of cases we accept the answer given.   There are other cases where people say they have forgotten their motive.   Other cases where you are puzzled immediately after you have done something and ask: "Why did I do this?"[3]   Suppose Taylor was in this state and I said: "Look here, Taylor.   The molecules in the sofa attract the molecules in your brain, etc. . . and so . . ."

18.   Suppose Taylor and I are walking along the river and Taylor stretches out his hand and pushes me in the river.   When I ask why he did this he says: "I was pointing out something to you", whereas the psycho-analyst says that Taylor subconsciously hated me.[4]   Suppose e.g. it often happened that when two people were walking along a river:

(1) they were talking amicably;

[1] We may give the process which led to it before. Or it may be what we now see would justify it.—R.

(It is not a natural usage of 'motive'.) You might say: 'He knows what he was doing, nobody else does.'—T.

[2] Thus 'reason' does not always mean the same thing. And similarly with 'motive'. 'Why did you do it?' One sometimes answers: 'Well, I said to myself: "I must see him because he is ill." '—actually remembering having said things to oneself. Or again, in many cases the motive is the justification we give on being asked—just that.—R.

[3] But is it clear why one should be puzzled?—R.

[4] A lot of things confirm this. At the same time a psycho-analyst has another explanation.—T. We might have evidence that the psycho-analyst's explanation is correct.—R.

(2) one was obviously pointing out something and pushed the other in the river;

(3) the person pushed in had a similarity with the father of the other person.

Here we have two explanations:

(1) He subconsciously hated the other man.

(2) He was pointing at something.

19. Both explanations may be correct. When would we say that Taylor's explanation was correct? When he had never shown any unfriendly feelings, when a church-steeple and I were in his field of vision, and Taylor was known to be truthful. But, under the same circumstances, the psycho-analyst's explanation may also be correct.[1] Here there are two motives—conscious and unconscious. The games played with the two motives are utterly different.[2] The explanations could in a sense be contradictory and yet both be correct. (Love and Hate.)[3]

20. This connects up with something that Freud does. Freud does something which seems to me immensely wrong. He gives what he calls an interpretation of dreams. In his book *The Interpretation of Dreams* he describes one dream which he calls a 'beautiful dream' ['Ein schöner Traum'—R].[4] A patient, after saying that she had had a beautiful dream, described a dream in which she descended from a height, saw flowers and shrubs, broke off the branch of a tree, etc. Freud shows what he calls the 'meaning' of the dream. The coarsest sexual stuff, bawdy of the worst kind—if you wish to call it that—bawdy from A to Z. We know what we mean by bawdy. A remark sounds to the uninitiated harmless, but the initiated, say, chuckle when they hear it. Freud says the dream is bawdy. *Is* it bawdy? He shows relations between the dream images and certain objects of a sexual nature. The relation he establishes is roughly this. By a chain of associations which comes naturally under certain circumstances, this

[1] He hated me because I reminded him of something. And the psychoanalyst's statement is then corroborated. *How* corroborated?—R.

[2] Utterly different things are done with the statement of conscious motive and with the statement of unconscious motive.—R.

[3] One could be love and one could be hatred.—R.

[4] Freud's 'Ein schöner Traum' (*Die Traumdeutung* Frankfurt: Fischer Bücherei, 1961, p. 240) does not contain the features of the 'beautiful dream' described here. But the dream which does contain them (the 'flowery dream'—'Blumentraum'—p. 289) is in fact described as 'beautiful' or 'pretty' ('schöne'): 'Der schöne Traum wollte der Träumerin nach der Deutung gar nicht mehr gefallen.'—Ed.

leads to that, etc.[1] Does this prove that the dream is what is
called bawdy? Obviously not. If a person talks bawdy he doesn't
say something which seems to him harmless, and is then psycho-
analysed.[2] Freud called this dream 'beautiful', putting 'beautiful'
in inverted commas. But *wasn't* the dream beautiful? I would
say to the patient: "Do these associations make the dream not
beautiful? It was beautiful.[3] Why shouldn't it be?" I would
say Freud had cheated the patient. Cf. scents made of things
having intolerable smells. Could we therefore say: "The 'best'
scent is really all sulphuric acid?"[4] Why did Freud give this
explanation at all? Two things people might say:

    (1) He wishes to explain everything nice in a nasty way,
        meaning almost that he is fond of bawdy. This is obviously
        not the case.

    (2) The connections he makes interest people immensely.
        They have a charm. It is charming[5] to destroy prejudice.

    21.   Cf. "If we boil Redpath at 200° C. all that is left when the
water vapour is gone is some ashes, etc.[6] This is all Redpath
really is." Saying this might have a certain charm, but would be
misleading to say the least.

    22.   The attraction of certain kinds of explanation is over-
whelming. At a given time the attraction of a certain kind of
explanation is greater than you can conceive.[7] In particular,
explanation of the kind 'This is really only this'.

    23.   There is a strong tendency to say: "We can't get round
the fact that this dream is really such and such."[8] It may be the
fact that the explanation is extremely repellent that drives you to
adopt it.

    24.   If someone says: "Why do you say it is really this?
Obviously it is not this at all", it is in fact even difficult to see it as
something else.

---

[1] From a flower to this, a tree to that, etc.—R.

[2] You don't say a person talks bawdy when his intention is innocent.—T.

[3] This is what is called beautiful.—T.

[4] If there is a connection between butyric acid which stinks and the best per-
fumes, could we on that account put 'the best perfume' in quotes.—T.

[5] To some people.—R.

[6] 'If we heat this man to 200 degrees Centigrade, the water evaporates . . .'—R.

[7] If you haven't just the right examples in mind.—T.

[8] If we see the connection of something like this beautiful dream to something
ugly . . .—R.

25. Here is an extremely interesting psychological phenomenon, that this ugly explanation makes you say you really had
these thoughts, whereas in any ordinary sense you really didn't.

(1) There is the process ['freier Einfall'—R] which connects
certain parts of the dream with certain objects.

(2) There is the process 'So this is what I meant'. There is a
maze for people to go astray in here.[1]

26. Suppose you were analysed when you had a stammer.
(1) You may say that that explanation [analysis—R] is correct
which cures the stammer. (2) If the stammer is not cured the
criterion may be the person analysed saying: "This explanation
is correct",[2] or agreeing that the explanation given him is correct.
(3) Another criterion is that according to certain rules of experience[3] the explanation given is the correct one, whether the person
to whom it is given adopts it or not.[4] Many of these explanations
are adopted because they have a peculiar charm. The picture of
people having subconscious thoughts has a charm. The idea of
an underworld, a secret cellar. Something hidden, uncanny. Cf.
Keller's two children putting a live fly in the head of a doll,
burying the doll and then running away.[5] (Why do we do this
sort of thing? This is the sort of thing we do do.) A lot of things
one is ready to believe because they are uncanny.

27. One of the most important things about an explanation
[in Physics R, T] is that it should work, that it should enable us
to predict something [successfully—T]. Physics is connected
with Engineering. The bridge must not fall down.

28. Freud says: "There are several instances (cf. Law) in the
mind."[6] Many of these explanations (i.e. of psycho-analysis) are
not borne out by experience, as an explanation in Physics is.[7] The

[1] These two need not go together. Either might work and the other not.—R.
[2] 'Oh yes, that's what I meant.'—R. Or you may say that the analogy is correct
which the person analysed agrees to.—T.
[3] Of explaining such phenomena.—R.
[4] Or you may say that the correct analogy is the accepted one. The one ordinarily
given.—T.
[5] Gottfried Keller (1819–1890). A Swiss poet, novelist and short-story writer.
The incident to which Wittgenstein refers occurs in *Romeo und Julia auf dem Dorfe*,
Werke V-VI, Berlin, 1889, p. 84.—Ed.
[6] If you look at what Freud says in explanation—not in his clinical procedure,
but, for instance, what we say about the different 'Instanzen' ('instances', in the sense
in which we speak of a court of higher instance) of the mind.—R.
[7] An explanation in a different sense often. Its attractiveness is important, more
important than in the case of an explanation in physics.—T.

C

attitude they express is important. They give us a picture which has a peculiar attraction for us.[1]

29. Freud has very intelligent reasons for saying what he says, great imagination and colossal prejudice, and prejudice which is very likely to mislead people.[2]

30. Suppose someone like Freud stresses enormously the importance of sexual motives:

(1) Sexual motives are immensely important.

(2) Often people have good reason to hide a sexual motive as a motive.[3]

31. Isn't this also a good reason for *admitting* sex as a motive for everything, for saying: "This is really at the bottom of everything"? Isn't it clear that a particular way of explaining can bring you to admit another thing. Suppose I show Redpath fifty cases where he admits a certain motive, twenty cases where this motive is an important link. I could make him admit it as a motive in all cases.[4]

32. Cf. The Darwin upheaval. One circle of admirers who said: "Of course", and another circle [of enemies—R] who said: "Of course not".[5] Why in the Hell should a man say 'of course'? (The idea was that of monocellular organisms becoming more and more complicated until they became mammals, men, etc.) Did anyone see this process happening? No. Has anyone seen it happening now? No. The evidence of breeding is just a drop in the bucket. But there were thousands of books in which this was said to be *the* obvious solution. People were *certain* on grounds which were extremely thin. Couldn't there have been an attitude which said: "I don't know. It is an interesting hypothesis which may eventually be well confirmed"?[6] This shows how you can be persuaded of a certain thing. In the end you

---

[1] This does not help us to *predict* anything, but it has a peculiar attraction.—R.

[2] People can be convinced of many things according to what you tell them.—R.

[3] It is disagreeable to have to admit it so often.—R.

[4] If you get him to admit that *this* is at the bottom of everything, is it therefore at the bottom of everything? All you can say is that you can bring certain people to think that it is.—T.

[5] What does their saying this mean?—T. We could say the same thing against both of them.—R.

[6] But people were immensely attracted by the unity of the theory, by the single principle—which was taken to be the obvious solution. The certainty ('of course') was created by the enormous charm of this unity. People could have said: '. . . Perhaps sometime we shall find grounds.' But hardly anyone said this; they were either sure that it was so, or sure that it was not so.—R.

forget entirely every question of verification, you are just sure
it must have been like that.

33. If you are led by psycho-analysis to say that really you
thought so and so or that really your motive was so and so, this
is not a matter of discovery, but of persuasion.[1] In a different
way you could have been persuaded of something different. Of
course, if psycho-analysis cures your stammer, it cures it, and that
is an achievement. One thinks of certain results of psycho-
analysis as a discovery Freud made, as apart from something
persuaded to you by a psycho-analyst, and I wish to say this is not
the case.

34. Those sentences have the form of persuasion in particular which say 'This is *really* this'. [This means—R] there are
certain differences which you have been persuaded to neglect.[2] It
reminds me of that marvellous motto: 'Everything is what it is
and not another thing.' The dream is not bawdy, it is something else.

35. I very often draw your attention to certain differences,
e.g. in these classes I tried to show you that Infinity is not so
mysterious as it looks. What I'm doing is also persuasion. If
someone says: "There is not a difference", and I say: "There is
a difference" I am persuading, I am saying "I don't want you to
look at it like that."[3] Suppose I wished to show how very misleading the expressions of Cantor are. You ask: "What do you
mean, it is misleading? Where does it lead you to?"

36. Jeans has written a book called *The Mysterious Universe*
and I loathe it and call it misleading. Take the title. This alone
I would call misleading.[4] Cf. Is the thumb-catcher deluded or
not?[5] Was Jeans deluded when he said it was mysterious? I
might say the title *The Mysterious Universe* includes a kind of idol
worship, the idol being Science and the Scientist.

[1] We are likely to think of a person's admitting in analysis that he thought so
and so as a kind of discovery which is independent of having been persuaded by a
psychoanalyst.—R.
[2] This means you are neglecting certain things and have been persuaded to
neglect them.—R.
[3] I am saying I want you to look at the thing in a different way.—T.
[4] But in what way is it misleading? Isn't it mysterious, or is it?—R.
[5] I have been talking about the game of 'thumb catching'. What's wrong with
that?—R. 'Thumb-catching': holding the right thumb, say, in the left hand, then
trying to grasp it with right hand. The thumb 'mysteriously' disappears before it can
be grasped.—Ed.

37.   I am in a sense making propaganda for one style of thinking as opposed to another. I am honestly disgusted with the other. Also I'm trying to state what I think. Nevertheless I'm saying: "For God's sake don't do this."[1] E.g. I pulled Ursell's proof to bits. But after I had done, he said that the proof had a charm for him. Here I could only say: "It has no charm for me. I loathe it."[2] Cf. the expression 'The Cardinal number of all Cardinal numbers'.

38.   Cf. Cantor wrote how marvellous it was that the mathematician could in his imagination [mind—T] transcend all limits.

39.   I would do my utmost to show it is this charm that makes one do it.[3] Being Mathematics or Physics it looks incontrovertible and this gives it a still greater charm. If we explain the surroundings of the expression we see that the thing could have been expressed in an entirely different way. I can put it in a way in which it will lose its charm for a great number of people and certainly will lose its charm for me.[4]

40.   How much we are doing is changing the style of thinking and how much I'm doing is changing the style of thinking and how much I'm doing is persuading people to change their style of thinking.

41.   (Much of what we are doing is a question of changing the style of thinking.)

IV

(From Rhees's Notes)

1.   Aesthetic puzzles—puzzles about the effects the arts have on us.[5]

Paradigm of the sciences is mechanics. If people imagine a

---

[1] I stop being puzzled and I persuade you to do something different.—T.

[2] Regarding Cantor's proofs—I would try to show that it is this charm which makes the proof attractive. (After I had discussed these proofs with Ursell, and he had agreed with me, he said: 'And still. . .')—R.

[3] I would do my utmost to show the effects of the charm, and of the associations of 'Mathematics'.—T.

[4] If I describe the surroundings of the proof, then you may see that the thing could have been expressed in an entirely different way; and then you see that the similarity of $\aleph_0$ and a cardinal number is very small. The matter can be put in a way which loses the charm it has for many people.—R.

[5] The puzzles which arise in aesthetics, which are puzzles arising from the effects the arts have, are not puzzles about how these things are caused.—S.

psychology, their ideal is a mechanics of the soul.[1] If we look at what actually corresponds to that, we find there are physical experiments and there are psychological experiments. There are laws of physics and there are laws—if you wish to be polite—of psychology. But in physics there are almost too many laws; in psychology there are hardly any. So, to talk about a mechanics of the soul is slightly funny.

2. But we can dream of predicting the reactions of human beings, say to works of art. If we imagine the dream realized, we'd not thereby have solved what we feel to be aesthetic puzzlements, although we may be able to predict that a certain line of poetry will, on a certain person, act in such and such a way. What we really want, to solve aesthetic puzzlements, is certain comparisons—grouping together of certain cases.[2]

There is a tendency to talk about the 'effect of a work of art'—feelings, images, etc.[3] Then it is natural to ask: "Why do you hear this minuet?", and there is a tendency to answer: "To get this and that effect." And doesn't the minuet itself matter?—hearing *this*: would another have done as well?

You could play a minuet once and get a lot out of it, and play the same minuet another time and get nothing out of it. But it doesn't follow that what you get out of it is then independent of the minuet. Cf. the mistake of thinking that the meaning or thought is just an accompaniment of the word, and the word doesn't matter. 'The sense of a proposition' is very similar to the business of 'an appreciation of art'. The idea that a sentence has a relation to an object, such that, whatever has this effect is the *sense* of the sentence. "What about a French sentence?—There is the same accompaniment, namely the *thought*."

A man may sing a song with expression and without expression. Then why not leave out the song—could you have the expression then?

[1] I suppose the paradigm of all science is mechanics, e.g. Newtonian mechanics. Psychology: Three laws for the soul.—S.

[2] A picture, 'Creation of Adam' by Michelangelo, comes to mind. I have a queer idea which could be expressed by: 'There is a tremendous *philosophy* behind this picture.'—S.

[3] Does that mean that if you gave a person the effects and removed the picture it would be all right? Surely (the) first thing is, you see the picture or say the words of a poem. Would a syringe which produces these effects on you do just as well as the picture?—S.

If a Frenchman says: "It is raining" in French and an Englishman also says it in English, it is not that something happens in both minds which is the real sense of 'It is raining'. We imagine something like *imagery*, which is the international language. Whereas in fact:

(1) Thinking (or imagery) is not an accompaniment of the words as they are spoken or heard;

(2) The sense—the thought 'It's raining'—is not even the words *with* the accompaniment of some sort of imagery.

It *is* the thought 'It's raining' only within the English language.[1]

3. If you ask: "What is the peculiar effect of these words?", in a sense you make a mistake. What if they had no effect at all? Aren't they peculiar words?

"Then why do we admire this and not that?" "I don't know."

Suppose I give you a pill

(1) which makes you draw a picture—perhaps 'The Creation of Adam';

(2) which gives you feelings in the stomach.

Which would you call the more *peculiar* effect? Certainly—that you draw just this picture. The feelings are pretty simple.

"Look at a face—what is important is its expression—not its colour, size, etc."

"Well give us the expression without the face."

The expression is not an *effect* of the face—on me or anyone. You could not say that if anything else had this effect, it would have the expression on this face.[2]

I want to make you sad. I show you a picture, and you are sad. This is the effect of this face.

4. The importance of our memory for the expression of a face. You may show me sticks at different times—one is shorter than the other. I may not remember that the other time it was longer. But I compare them, and this shows me they are not the same.

[1] (You could call the music the scraping of the fiddles, etc., and the effect the noises we hear, but aren't the auditory impressions as important as the visual one?)

Thinking is not even speaking with accompaniment, noises accompanied with whatever may be, is not the sort 'It rains' at all, but is within English language. A Chinaman who makes noise 'It rains' with same accompaniments—Does he think 'It rains'?—S.

[2] Face is not a means to produce the expression.—S.

I may draw you a face. Then at another time I draw another face. You say: "That's not the same face."—but you can't say whether the eyes are closer together, or mouth longer [eyes bigger or nose longer—S], or anything of this sort. "It looks different, somehow."[1]

This is enormously important for all philosophy.

5. If I draw a meaningless curve [squiggle—S]

and then draw another later, pretty much like it, you would not know the difference. But if I draw this peculiar thing which I call a face, and then draw one slightly different, you will know at once there is a difference.

Recognising an expression. Architecture:—draw a door —"Slightly too large." You might say: "He has an excellent eye for measurement." No—he sees it hasn't the right expression—it doesn't make the right gesture.[2]

If you showed me a stick of different length, I'd not have known. Also, in this case I don't make queer gestures and noise; but I do when I see a door or a face.

I say, e.g. of a smile: "It wasn't quite genuine."

"Oh bosh, the lips were parted only 1/1000th of an inch too much. Does it matter?"

"Yes."

"Then it is because of certain consequences."

But not only that: the reaction is different.

We can give the history of the matter—we react so because it is a *human* face. But apart from history—our reaction to these lines is entirely different from our reaction to any other lines. Two faces might have the same expression. Say they are both sad. But if I say: "It has exactly *this* expression. . ." . . .[3]

---

[1] It is (the) fact of remembering a facial expression.—S.

[2] Not a matter of measurement.—S.

[3] Can squiggle have same effect as picture of a face? (1) Brothers had same sad expression. (2) It had this expression, photograph and gesture.—S.

6. I draw a few dashes with a pencil and paper, and then ask: "Who is this?" and get the answer: "It is Napoleon". We have never been taught to call these marks, 'Napoleon'.

The phenomenon is similar to that of weighing in a balance. I can easily distinguish between a few scratches, on the one hand, and a picture of a man properly drawn, on the other. No one would say: "This is the same as that" in one sense. But, on the other hand, we say: "That's Napoleon". On one peculiar [particular?] balance we say: "This is the same as that". On one balance the audience easily distinguishes between the face of the actor and the face of Lloyd George.

All have learnt the use of '='. And suddenly they use it in a peculiar way. They say: "This is Lloyd George," although in another sense there is no similarity. An equality which we could call the 'equality of expression'. We have learnt the use of 'the same'. Suddenly we automatically use 'the same' when there is not similarity of length, weight or anything of the sort.[1]

In a lecture on description Wittgenstein raised another point about similarity which deserves to be quoted and might be included here—Ed. 'Take a case where you notice a peculiarity in poems of one poet. You can sometimes find the similarity between the style of a musician and the style of a poet who lived at the same time, or a painter. Take Brahms and Keller. I often found that certain themes of Brahms were extremely Kellerian. This was extraordinarily striking. First I said this to people. You might say: "What would be the interest of such an utterance?" The interest partly lay in that they lived at the same time.

If I had said he was Shakespearean or Miltonian, this might have had no interest or an entirely different one. If I had constantly wanted to say: "This is Shakespearean" of a certain theme, this would have had little or no interest. It wouldn't connect up with anything. 'This word ('Shakespearean') forces itself on me.' Did I have a certain scene in mind? If I say this theme of Brahms is extremely Kellerian, the interest this has is first that these two lived at the same time. Also that you can say the same sort of things of both of them—the culture of the time in which they lived. If I say this, this comes to an objective interest. The interest might be that my words suggest a hidden connection.

E.g. Here you actually have a case different from that of faces. With faces you can generally soon find something which makes you say: "Yes that's what made them so similar." Whereas I couldn't say now what it is that made Brahms similar to Keller. Nevertheless, I find that utterance of mine interesting. It derives its main interest from the fact that these two lived [at the same time]. "That was [wasn't] written before Wagner." The interest of this statement would lie in the fact that on the whole such statements are true when I make them. One can actually judge when a piece of poetry was written by hearing it, by the style. You could imagine this was impossible, if people in 1850 wrote the same way as in 1750, but you could still imagine people saying: "I am sure that was written in 1850." Cf. [A man on a railway journey to Liverpool saying,] "I am sure Exeter is in that direction." '—S.

[1] We use 'agreed' in another way. This is equality and is equality of expression. We suddenly, automatically, use 'the same' when it's not length, or breadth, etc., although we've learnt it in connection with these.—S.

The most exact description of my feelings here would be that I say: "Oh, that's Lloyd George!"[1]

Suppose the most exact description of a feeling is "stomach-ache". But why isn't the most important description of feeling that you say: "Oh, this is the same as that!"?

7. Here is the point of Behaviorism. It isn't that they deny there are feelings. But they say our description of behaviour *is* our description of feelings.

"What did he feel when he said: 'Duncan is in his grave'?" Can I describe his feelings better than by describing how he said it?[2] All other descriptions are crude compared with a description of the gesture he made, the tone of voice with which he made it.

What is a description of feeling at all? What is a description of pain?[3]

Discussion of a comedian doing imitations, sketches. Suppose you want to describe the experience of the audience— why not describe first of all what they saw? Then perhaps that they shook with laughter, then what they said.[4]

"This can't be a description of their feelings." One says this because one is thinking of their organic feelings—tension of the muscles in their chest, etc. This would obviously be an experience. But it doesn't seem half as important as the fact that they said so and so. One thinks of a description of experience not as a description of action, but as of a description of pain or organic feelings.

Cf. what we said about the way in which fashions arise: whether he feels so and so when he cuts lapel of coat bigger. But that he *cuts* it in this way, etc.[5]—this is the most important part of the experience.

[1] Important thing is I say: 'Yes, this is Drury.' If you wish to describe feelings, the best way is to describe reactions. Saying 'This is Drury' is the most exact description of feelings I can give at all. Idea that most exact way of describing is by feelings in the stomach.—S.

[2] Can I describe his feelings better than (by) imitating the way he said it? Isn't this most impressive?—S.

[3] 'He felt this' (touching head).—S.

[4] Suppose I said: 'The crowd roared with laughter,' without describing what they were laughing at; describing what they were laughing at but not them laughing. Why not first describe what they saw, then what they did or said, then feelings?—S.

[5] . . . his making it bigger or saying: 'No, no, no?'—S.

8. "Is the most important impression which a picture produces a visual impression or not?"

[(1)] "No. Because you can do things which visually change the picture and yet not change the impression." This sounds as though one wished to say it wasn't an impression of the eyes: an effect, but not a purely visual effect.

[(2)] "But it *is* a visual impression". Only these are the features of the visual impression which matter, and not the others.

Suppose [someone says]: "Associations are what matter —change it slightly and it no longer has the same associations."

But can you separate the associations from the picture, and have the same thing? You can't say: "That's just as good as the other: it gives me the same associations."

9. You *could* select either of two poems to remind you of death, say. But supposing you had read a poem and admired it, could you say: "Oh, read the other, it will do the same"?

How do we use poetry? Does it play this role—that we say such a thing as: "Here is something just as good. . . ."?

Imagine an entirely different civilization.[1] Here there is something you might call music, since it has notes. They treat music like this: certain music makes them walk like this. They play a record to do this. One says: "I need this record now. Oh no, take the other, it is just as good."

If I admire a minuet I can't say: "Take another. It does the same thing." What do you mean? It *is* not the same.[2]

If someone talks bosh, imagine a case in which it is not bosh. The moment you imagine it, you see at once it is not like that in our case. We *don't* read poetry to get associations. We don't happen to, but we might.

10. Two schools:

(1) "What matters is the patches of colour [and lines—S]."

(2) "What matters is the expression on these faces."

In a sense, these two don't contradict one another. Only (1) doesn't make clear that the different patches have different

---

[1]Another culture where music makes them do different things. Cf. (the) role music plays with us with the rôle music plays with others. One can't say now: 'Play Mozart it does just as well.'—S.

[2] Cf. language where producing pictures by words is important thing. You can see how our language is not like that.

Poems, sea, sea-picture. Ask him. Show him the difference, etc.—S.

importance, and that different *alterations* have totally different effects: some make all the difference in the world.

"A picture must be good even if you look at it upside down." Then, the smile may not be noticeable.

[Suppose you said:] "That tiny smile by which you change the kindly smile into an ironic one, is not a purely visual difference," (Cf. a picture of a monk looking at a vision of the Virgin Mary.) [Suppose you said:] "It changes your whole attitude towards the picture." This may be entirely true. How would this be expressed? Perhaps by the smile you make. The one picture might be blasphemous; with the other you are as you might be in a church. Your attitude might be in the one case that you stand before it almost in prayer, in the other case almost leering· This is a difference of attitude.

"Well, there you are. It is all the attitude." But you could have these attitudes without a picture. They are important—certainly.

11. "You have given a rough description of the attitude. What you have to describe is something more subtle." But if we describe the attitude more exactly, how do you know that this is the essential thing for *this* picture—that all this must always be present?

Don't imagine a description which you have never heard, which describes an attitude in unheard of detail. For you know nothing about such an attitude. We have no idea of such an attitude.

An attitude is pretty well described by the position of the body. This is a good description. But accurate? In a way it is inaccurate. "But if you knew all the muscular sensations, you would point to just those which matter."[1] I don't know them and I don't know what such a description would be like.[2] This is not what we mean by description. Don't imagine an imaginary kind of description of which you really have no idea.

If you say 'description of attitude', tell us what you call a description of attitude, then you will see the attitude matters. Some changes change the attitude—We say: "the whole thing is changed."

[1] Who says he always must have this feeling in this muscle? He distinguishes between looking at the picture and looking at this, but he does not distinguish between his muscular feelings.—S.

[2] I can describe how a man stands and then I can describe the picture. Man who makes twelve changes in Michelangelo.—S.

12.   Associations also [enormously] matter. These are shown chiefly by the things we say. We call this 'God the Father', the other 'Adam'; we could go on: "That comes in the Bible, etc." Is this all that matters? We could have all these associations with a different picture, and would still want to see *this* picture.

"That means the chief impression is the visual impression." Yes, it's the picture which seems to matter most. Associations may vary, attitudes may vary, but change the picture ever so slightly, and you won't want to look at it any more.

The craving for simplicity. [People would like to say:] "What really matters is only the colours." You say this mostly because you wish it to be the case. If your explanation is complicated, it is disagreeable, especially if you don't have strong feelings about the thing itself.

FROM A LECTURE BELONGING TO A COURSE OF LECTURES ON DESCRIPTION

One of the most interesting points which the question of not being able to describe is connected with, [is that] the impression which a certain verse or bar in music gives you is indescribable. "I don't know what it is... Look at this transition. .... What is it? ...." I think you would say it gives you experiences which can't be described. First of all it is, of course, not true that whenever we hear a piece of music or a line of poetry which impresses us greatly, we say: "This is indescribable". But it is true that again and again we do feel inclined to say: "I can't describe my experience". I have in mind a case that saying one is incapable of describing comes from being intrigued and *wanting* to describe, asking oneself: "What is this? What's he doing, wanting to do here?—Gosh, if I could only say what he's doing here."

Very many people have the feeling: "I can make a gesture but that's all". One example is that you say of a certain phrase of music that it draws a conclusion, "Though I couldn't say for my life why it is a 'therefore'!" You say in this case that it is indescribable. But this does not mean that you may not one day say that something is a *description*. You may one day find the *word* or you find a verse that fits it. "It is as though he said: ' . . .'," and you have a verse. And now perhaps you say: "And now I understand it."

If you say: "We haven't got the technique" (I. A. Richards), what in such a case are we entitled to call such a description? You might say some such thing as: "Well, now, if you hear this piece of music, you get certain sense impressions. Certain images, certain organic feelings, emotions, etc.", meanings, "we still don't know how to analyse this impression."

The mistake seems to me in the idea of description. I said before, with some people, me especially, the expression of an emotion in music, say, is a certain gesture. If I make a certain gesture. . . . "It is quite obvious that you have certain kinesthetic feelings. It means to you certain kinesthetic feelings." Which ones? How can you describe them? Except, perhaps, just by the gesture?

Suppose you said: "This phrase in music always makes me make one peculiar gesture." A painter might draw this gesture. A man, instead of making a gesture, would draw a gesture. For him it would be an expression to draw this gesture, or a face going with it, as for me it is to make a gesture. "Wittgenstein, you talk as if this phrase gave you sensations you couldn't describe. All you get is sensations in your muscles." This is utterly misleading. We look up muscles in a book on anatomy, we press certain parts and give these sensations names, 'A', 'B', 'C', etc. All that would be needed for a piece of music would be the description 'A', etc., giving the sensations in each muscle. It now seems as though you could do something like this. What a man sees can generally be described. Names of colours etc. One assumes at least a picture can be described. One goes on and says not only a visual picture but picture of Kinesthetic Sensations.

By the way, in what way is it wrong for a picture? Suppose we said, that we cannot describe in words the expression of God in Michelangelo's 'Adam'. "But this is only a matter of technique, because if we drew a lattice-work over his face, numbered,

I would just write down numbers and you might say: "My God! It's grand." It wouldn't be any description. You wouldn't say such a thing at all. It would only be a description if you could paint (act?) according to this picture, which, of course, is conceivable. But this would show that you can't at all transmit the impression by words, but you'd have again to paint.

Could you imagine: it is an odd fact that we sometimes imitate someone else? I remember walking in the street and saying: "I am now walking exactly like Russell." You might say it was a kinesthetic sensation. Very queer.

A person who imitates another's face doesn't do it before a mirror but it is a fact that there is such a thing as saying: "The face is so and so."

Suppose I make a gesture and I think the gesture characteristic for the impression I get. Suppose I gave the gesture by co-ordinates and I wish to make it clear to Mr. Lewy. He might have to make an analogous gesture. His muscles, hands, etc., are differently shaped. So in one sense, he can't copy and in another sense he can. What are we to regard as the copy? "It will depend on how such muscles contract." But how on earth are you to know? If I make a gesture, and you are good imitators, these gestures will have to be similar, but different; the shape of the fingers, etc., is different. The criterion for its being this gesture will be the clicking of it in you. You say: "Now this." To say what's similar is impossible (to say). Each one makes a gesture immediately and says: "That's the one."

If I wish to convey an impression to Mr. Lewy, it might only be made in this way, that he copies my gesture. Then what about this technique of describing kinesthetic sensations? This isn't co-ordinates; it is something else: imitating the person. "Wittgenstein, if you make a gesture, all you get are certain kinesthetic sensations." It is not at all clear in what case we do say we have conveyed them. But it may, e.g., be by what we call 'imitating'.

Whether it is this will depend on. . . .

"There is a phenomenon, the following: if you give me a piece of music and ask me in what tempo it ought to be played, I may or may not be absolutely certain. "Perhaps, like this . . . I don't know." Or "Like this", telling you exactly what tempo it is to be. I always insist on one tempo, not necessarily the same. In the other case I am uncertain. Suppose the question were to transmit to you a certain impression I get of a piece of music. That might depend on the fact that a certain number of you, on my playing it to you, (that you) "get it", 'get hold of it'. What does it consist in to get hold of a tune or a piece of poetry?

You may read a stanza. I let you all read it. Everyone reads it slightly differently. I get the definite impression that "None of them has got hold of it." Suppose then I read it out to you and say: "Look, this is how it ought to be". Then four of you read this stanza, no one exactly like the other, but in such a way that I say: "Each one is exactly certain of himself." This is a phenomenon, being certain of yourself, reading it in *one way only*. He is absolutely exact as to what pause to make. I might say in this case that you four have got hold of it. I would have conveyed something to you. I would perfectly correctly say, that I have exactly conveyed to you the exact experience I had.

But what about the technique of imagery, etc.? This (convention/communication/description) is not based on copying me exactly. If I had a chronometer by which I can measure exactly the interval between the vowels, they may not be the same but entirely different.

If someone says: "We lack this technique", he presupposes that, if we had it, we would have a new expression, a new way of transmitting, not the old one. But how does he know that if we describe in the new way—suppose I had a way of describing kinesthetic sensations or way of describing gestures—I get the same as I got if I transmit gesture. Suppose I said: "I get a little tickling there" [running finger down hand]. Suppose I had six ticklings and I had a method of producing each one. Suppose I had instruments attached to my nerves in such a way that an electric current going through the nerves was measured by the instrument. You get an instrument reading. "Now I'll represent this in Mr. Lewy." But would this be the representation we want? I might read a stanza and you might say: "Wittgenstein obviously has got hold of it. He had got my interpretation." Mr. Lewy reads it and you say the same. But voice, strength, etc., are different. "My interpretation is that which produces the same kinesthetic impressions." But how do you know? This simply isn't an analysis at all. We have one way of comparing and if you say: "And also we could get a scientific one," I'd ask: "Yes, but what makes you think that these will go parallel at all?"

CONVERSATIONS ON FREUD

In these discussions Wittgenstein was critical of Freud. But he was also bringing out how much there is in what Freud says about the notion of "dream symbolism", for instance, or the suggestion that in dreaming I am—in some sense—'saying something'. He was trying to separate what is valuable in Freud from that 'way of thinking' which he wanted to combat.

He told me that when he was in Cambridge before 1914 he had thought psychology a waste of time. (Although he had not ignored it. I heard him explain the Weber-Fechner law to a student in a way that cannot have come simply from reading Meinong's article or from discussions with Russell.) "Then some years later I happened to read something by Freud, and I sat up in surprise. Here was someone who had something to say." I think this was soon after 1919. And for the rest of his life Freud was one of the few authors he thought worth reading. He would speak of himself—at the period of these discussions—as "a disciple of Freud" and "a follower of Freud".

He admired Freud for the observations and suggestions in his writings; for "having something to say" even where, in Wittgenstein's view, he was wrong. On the other hand, he thought the enormous influence of psychoanalysis in Europe and America was harmful—"although it will take a long time before we lose our subservience to it". To learn from Freud you have to be critical; and psychoanalysis generally prevents this.

I spoke of the harm it does to writing when an author tries to bring psychoanalysis into the story. "Of course," he said, "There's nothing worse." He was ready to illustrate what Freud meant by referring to a story; but then the story had been written independently. Once when Wittgenstein was recounting something Freud had said and the advice he had given someone, one of us said that this advice did not seem very wise. "Oh certainly not," said Wittgenstein. "But wisdom is something I never would expect from Freud. Cleverness, certainly; but not wisdom." Wisdom was something he did admire in his favourite story writers—in Gottfried Keller, for instance. The kind of criticism

D

which would help in studying Freud, would have to go deep; and it is not common.

RUSH RHEES.

WITTGENSTEIN (notes by R. R. after a conversation, Summer 1942).

When we are studying psychology we may feel there is something unsatisfactory, some difficulty about the whole subject or study—because we are taking physics as our ideal science. We think of formulating laws as in physics. And then we find we cannot use the same sort of 'metric', the same ideas of measurement as in physics. This is especially clear when we try to describe appearances: the least noticeable differences of colours; the least noticeable differences of length, and so on. Here it seems that we cannot say: "If A=B, and B=C, then A=C," for instance. And this sort of trouble goes all through the subject.

Or suppose you want to speak of causality in the operation of feelings. "Determinism applies to the mind as truly as to physical things." This is obscure because when we think of causal laws in physical things we think of *experiments*. We have nothing like this in connexion with feelings and motivation. And yet psychologists wants to say: "There *must* be some law"—although no law has been found. (Freud: "Do you want to say, gentlemen, that changes in mental phenomena are guided by *chance*?") Whereas to me the fact that there *aren't* actually any such laws seems important.

Freud's theory of dreams. He wants to say that whatever happens in a dream will be found to be connected with some wish which analysis can bring to light. But this procedure of free association and so on is queer, because Freud never shows how we know where to stop—where is the right solution. Sometimes he says that the right solution, or the right analysis, is the one which satisfies the patient. Sometimes he says that the doctor knows what the right solution or analysis of the dream is whereas the patient doesn't: the doctor can say that the patient is wrong.

The reason why he calls one sort of analysis the right one, does not seem to be a matter of evidence. Neither is the proposition that hallucinations, and so dreams, are wish fulfilments.

Suppose a starving man has an hallucination of food. Freud wants to say the hallucination of anything requires tremendous energy: it is not something that could normally happen, but the energy is provided in the exceptional circumstances where a man's wish for food is overpowering. This is a *speculation*. It is the sort of explanation we are inclined to accept. It is not put forward as a result of detailed examination of varieties of hallucinations.

Freud in his analysis provides explanations which many people are inclined to accept. He emphasizes that people are *dis*-inclined to accept them. But if the explanation is one which people are disinclined to accept, it is highly probable that it is also one which they are *inclined* to accept. And this is what Freud had actually brought out. Take Freud's view that anxiety is always a repetition in some way of the anxiety we felt at birth. He does not establish this by reference to evidence—for he could not do so. But it is an idea which has a marked attraction. It has the attraction which mythological explanations have, explanations which say that this is all a repetition of something that has happened before. And when people do accept or adopt this, then certain things seem much clearer and easier for them. So it is with the notion of the unconscious also. Freud does claim to find evidence in memories brought to light in analysis. But at a certain stage it is not clear how far such memories are due to the analyst. In any case, do they show that the anxiety was necessarily a repetition of the original anxiety?

Symbolizing in dreams. The idea of a dream language. Think of recognizing a painting as a dream. I (L.W.) was once looking at an exhibition of paintings by a young woman artist in Vienna. There was one painting of a bare room, like a cellar. Two men in top hats were sitting on chairs. Nothing else. And the title: "Besuch" ("Visit"). When I saw this I said at once "This is a dream", (My sister described the picture to Freud, and he said 'Oh yes, that is quite a common dream'—connected with virginity.) Note that the title is what clinches it as a dream—by which I do not mean that anything like this was dreamt by the painter while asleep. You would not say of *every* painting 'This is a dream'. And this does show that there is something like a dream language.

Freud mentions various symbols: top hats are regularly phallic symbols, wooden things like tables are women, etc. His historical explanation of these symbols is absurd. We might say it is not needed anyway: it is the most natural thing in the world that a table should be that sort of symbol.

But dreaming—using this sort of language—although it *may* be used to refer to a woman or to a phallus, may *also* be used not to refer to that at all. If some activity is shown to be carried out often for a certain purpose—striking someone to inflict pain—then a hundred to one it is also carried out under other circumstances *not* for that purpose. He may just want to strike him without thinking of inflicting pain at all. The fact that we are inclined to recognize the hat as a phallic symbol does not mean that the artist was necessarily referring to a phallus in any way when she painted it.

Consider the difficulty that if a symbol in a dream is not understood, it does not seem to be a symbol at all. So why call it one? But suppose I have a dream and accept a certain interpretation of it. *Then*—when I superimpose the interpretation on the dream—I can say "Oh yes, the table obviously corresponds to the woman, this to that etc."

I might be making scratches on the wall. It seems in a way like writing, but it is not a writing which either I or anyone else would recognize or understand. So we say I'm doodling. Then an analyst begins to ask me questions, trace associations and so on; and we come to an explanation of why I'm doing this. We may then correlate various scratches which I make with various elements in the interpretation. And we may then refer to the doodling as a kind of writing, as using a kind of language, although it was not understood by anyone.

Freud is constantly claiming to be scientific. But what he gives is *speculation*—something prior even to the formation of an hypothesis.

He speaks of overcoming resistance. One "instance" is deluded by another "instance". (In the sense in which we speak of "a court of higher instance" with authority to overrule the judgment of the lower court. RR.) The analyst is supposed to be stronger, able to combat and overcome the delusion of the instance. But there is no way of showing that the whole result of analysis may not be "delusion". It is something which people are inclined to accept and which makes it easier for them to go certain ways:

it makes certain ways of behaving and thinking natural for them. They have given up one way of thinking and adopted another.

Can we say we have laid bare the essential nature of mind? "Concept formation". Couldn't the whole thing have been differently treated?

WITTGENSTEIN (notes following conversations in 1943; Rush Rhees).
DREAMS. The interpretation of dreams. Symbolism.

When Freud speaks of certain images—say the image of a hat—as symbols, or when he says the image "means" so and so, he is speaking of interpretation; and of what the dreamer can be brought to accept as an interpretation.

It is characteristic of dreams that often they seem to the dreamer to call for an interpretation. One is hardly ever inclined to write down a day dream, or recount it to someone else, or to ask "What does it mean?" But dreams do seem to have something puzzling and in a special way interesting about them—so that we want an interpretation of them. (They were often regarded as messages.)

There seems to be something in dream images that has a certain resemblance to the signs of a language. As a series of marks on paper or on sand might have. There might be no mark which we recognized as a conventional sign in any alphabet we knew, and yet we might have a strong feeling that they must be a language of some sort: that they mean something. There is a cathedral in Moscow with five spires. On each of these there is a different sort of curving configuration. One gets the strong impression that these different shapes and arrangements must mean something.

When a dream is interpreted we might say that it is fitted into a context in which it ceases to be puzzling. In a sense the dreamer re-dreams his dream in surroundings such that its aspect changes. It is as though we were presented with a bit of canvas on which were painted a hand and a part of a face and certain other shapes, arranged in a puzzling and incongruous manner. Suppose this bit is surrounded by considerable stretches of blank canvas, and that we now paint in forms—say an arm, a trunk, etc.—leading up to and fitting on to the shapes on the original bit; and that the result is that we say: "Ah, now I see why it is like that, how it all comes to be arranged in that way, and what these various bits are . . ." and so on.

Mixed up with the shapes on the original bit of canvas there might be certain forms of which we should say that they do not join on to further figures in the wider canvas; they are not parts of bodies or trees, etc., but bits of writing. We might say this of a snake, perhaps, or a hat or some such. (These would be like the configurations of the Moscow cathedral.)

What is done in interpreting dreams is not all of one sort. There is a work of interpretation which, so to speak, still belongs to the dream itself. In considering what a dream is, it is important to consider what happens to it, the way its aspect changes when it is brought into relation with other things remembered, for instance. On first awaking a dream may impress one in various ways. One may be terrified and anxious; or when one has written the dream down one may have a certain sort of thrill, feel a very lively interest in it, feel intrigued by it. If one now remembers certain events in the previous day and connects what was dreamed with these, this already makes a difference, changes the aspect of the dream. If reflecting on the dream then leads one to remember certain things in early childhood, this will give it a different aspect still. And so on. (All this is connected with what was said about dreaming the dream over again. It still belongs to the dream, in a way.)

On the other hand, one might form an hypothesis. On reading the report of the dream, one might predict that the dreamer can be brought to recall such and such memories. And this hypothesis might or might not be verified. This might be called a scientific treatment of the dream.

Freier Einfall and wish fulfilments. There are various criteria for the right interpretation: e.g., (1) what the analyst says or predicts, on the basis of his previous experience; (2) what the dreamer is led to by *freier Einfall*. It would be interesting and important if these two generally coincided. But it would be queer to claim (as Freud seems to) that they *must always* coincide.

What goes on in *freier Einfall* is probably conditioned by a whole host of circumstances. There seems to be no reason for saying that it must be conditioned only by the sort of wish in which the analyst is interested and of which he has reason to say that it must have been playing a part. If you want to complete what seems to be a fragment of a picture, you might be advised to give up trying to think hard about what is the most likely way the picture went, and instead simply to stare at the picture and make whatever dash first comes into your mind, without thinking. This might in many cases be very fruitful advice to give. But it would be astonishing if it *always* produced the best results. What dashes you make, is likely to be conditioned by everything that is going on about you and within you. And if I knew one of the factors present, this could not tell me with certainty what dash you were going to make.

To say that dreams are wish fulfilments is very important chiefly because it points to the sort of interpretation that is wanted —the sort of thing that would be an interpretation of a dream. As contrasted with an interpretation which said that dreams were simply memories of what had happened, for instance. (We don't feel that memories call for an interpretation in the same way as we feel this about dreams.) And some dreams obviously are wish fulfilments; such as the sexual dreams of adults, for instance. But it seems muddled to say that *all* dreams are hallucinated wish fulfilments. (Freud very commonly gives what we might call a sexual interpretation. But it is interesting that among all the reports of dreams which he gives, there is not a single example of a straightforward sexual dream. Yet these are common as rain.) Partly because this doesn't seem to fit with dreams that spring from fear rather than from longing. Partly because the majority of dreams Freud considers have to be regarded as *camouflaged* wish fulfilments; and in this case they simply don't fulfil the wish. Ex hypothesi the wish is not allowed to be fulfilled, and something else is hallucinated instead. If the wish is cheated in this way, then the dream can hardly be called a fulfilment of it. Also it becomes impossible to say whether it is the wish or the censor that is cheated. Apparently both are, and the result is that neither is satisfied. So that the dream is not an hallucinated satisfaction of anything.

It is probable that there are many different sorts of dreams, and that there is no single line of explanation for all of them. Just as there are many different sorts of jokes. Or just as there are many different sorts of language.

Freud was influenced by the 19th century idea of dynamics—an idea which has influenced the whole treatment of psychology. He wanted to find some one explanation which would show what dreaming is. He wanted to find the *essence* of dreaming. And he would have rejected any suggestion that he might be partly right but not altogether so. If he was partly wrong, that would have meant for him that he was wrong altogether—that he had not really found the essence of dreaming.

WITTGENSTEIN. (Notes following conversations, 1943. R.R.)

Whether a dream is a thought. Whether dreaming is thinking about something.

Suppose you look on a dream as a kind of language. A way of saying something, or a way of symbolizing something. There might be a regular symbolism, not necessarily alphabetical—it might be like Chinese, say. We might then find a way of translating this symbolism into the language of ordinary speech, ordinary thoughts. But then the translation ought to be possible both ways. It ought to be possible by employing the same technique to translate ordinary thoughts into dream language. As Freud recognizes, this never is done and cannot be done. So we might question whether dreaming is a way of thinking something, whether it is a language at all.

Obviously there are certain similarities with language.

Suppose there were a picture in a comic paper, dated shortly after the last war. It might contain one figure of which you would say it was obviously a caricature of Churchill, another figure marked somehow with a hammer and sickle so that you would say it was obviously supposed to be Russia. Suppose the title of the picture was lacking. Still you might be sure that, in view of two figures mentioned, the whole picture was obviously trying to make some point about the political situation at that time.

The question is whether you would always be justified in assuming that there is some one joke or some one point which is *the* point which the cartoon is making. Perhaps even the picture as a whole has no "right interpretation" at all. You might say:

"There are indications—such as the two figures mentioned—which suggest that it has." And I might answer that perhaps these indications are all that there is. Once you have got an interpretation of these two figures, there may be no ground for saying that there *must* be an interpretation of the whole thing or of every detail of it on similar lines.

The situation may be similar in dreams.

Freud would ask: "What made you hallucinate that situation at all?" One might answer that there need not have been anything that *made* me hallucinate it.

Freud seems to have certain prejudices about when an interpretation could be regarded as complete—and so about when it still requires completion, when further interpretation is needed. Suppose someone were ignorant of the tradition among sculptors of making busts. If he then came upon the finished bust of some man, he might say that obviously this is a fragment and that there must have been other parts belonging to it, making it a whole body.

Suppose you recognized certain things in the dream which can be interpreted in the Freudian manner. Is there any ground at all for assuming that there must be an interpretation for everything else in the dream as well? that it makes any sense to ask what is the right interpretation of the other things there?

Freud asks "Are you asking me to believe that there is anything which happens without a cause?" But this means nothing. If under 'cause' you include things like physiological causes, then we know nothing about these, and in any case they are not relevant to the question of interpretation. Certainly you can't argue from Freud's question to the proposition that everything in the dream must have a cause in the sense of some past event with which it is connected by association in that way.

Suppose we were to regard a dream as a kind of game which the dreamer played. (And by the way, there is no one cause or one reason why children always play. This is where theories of play generally go wrong.) There might be a game in which paper figures were put together to form a story, or at any rate were somehow assembled. The materials might be collected and stored in a scrap-book, full of pictures and anecdotes. The child might then take various bits from the scrap-book to put into the construction; and he might take a considerable picture because it had something in it which he wanted and he might just include the rest because it was there.

Compare the question of why we dream and why we write stories. Not everything in the story is allegorical. What would be meant by trying to explain why he has written just that story in just that way?

There is no one reason why people talk. A small child babbles often just for the pleasure of making noises. This is also one reason why adults talk. And there are countless others.

Freud seems constantly to be influenced by the thought that a hallucination is something requiring a tremendous mental force—*seelische Kraft*. 'Ein Traum findet sich niemals mit Halbheiten ab.' And he thinks that the only force strong enough to produce the hallucinations of dreams is to be found in the deep wishes of early childhood. One might question this. Supposing it is true that hallucinations in waking state require an extraordinary mental force—why should not dream hallucinations be the perfectly normal thing in sleep, not requiring any extraordinary force at all?

(Compare the question: "Why do we punish criminals? Is it from a desire for revenge? Is it in order to prevent a repetition of the crime?" And so on. The truth is that there is no one reason. There is the institution of punishing criminals. Different people support this for different reasons, and for different reasons in different cases and at different times. Some people support it out of a desire for revenge, some perhaps out of a desire for justice, some out of a wish to prevent a repetition of the crime, and so on. And so punishments are carried out.)

WITTGENSTEIN (notes following conversation, 1946 R.R.)

I have been going through Freud's "Interpretation of Dreams" with H. And it has made me feel how much this whole way of thinking wants combatting.

If I take any one of the dream reports (reports of his own dreams) which Freud gives, I can by the use of free association arrive at the same results as those he reaches in his analysis— although it was not my dream. And the association will proceed through my own experiences and so on.

The fact is that whenever you are preoccupied with something, with some trouble or with some problem which is a big thing in your life—as sex is, for instance—then no matter what you start from, the association will lead finally and inevitably back to that same theme. Freud remarks on how, after the analysis of it, the dream appears so very logical. And of course it does.

You could start with any of the objects on this table—which certainly are not put there through your dream activity—and you could find that they all could be connected in a pattern like that; and the pattern would be logical in the same way.

One may be able to discover certain things about oneself by this sort of free association, but it does not explain why the dream occurred.

Freud refers to various ancient myths in these connexions, and claims that his researches have now explained how it came about that anybody should think or propound a myth of that sort.

Whereas in fact Freud has done something different. He has not given a scientific explanation of the ancient myth. What he has done is to propound a new myth. The attractiveness of the suggestion, for instance, that all anxiety is a repetition of the anxiety of the birth trauma, is just the attractiveness of a mythology. "It is all the outcome of something that happened long ago." Almost like referring to a totem.

Much the same could be said of the notion of an 'Urszene'. This often has the attractiveness of giving a sort of tragic pattern to one's life. It is all the repetition of the same pattern which was settled long ago. Like a tragic figure carrying out the decrees under which the fates had placed him at birth. Many people have, at some period, serious trouble in their lives—so serious as to lead to thoughts of suicide. This is likely to appear to one as something nasty, as a situation which is too foul to be a subject of a tragedy. And it may then be an immense relief if it can be shown that one's life has the pattern rather of a tragedy—the tragic working out and repetition of a pattern which was determined by the primal scene.

There is of course the difficulty of determining what scene is the primal scene—whether it is the scene which the patient recognizes as such, or whether it is the one whose recollection effects the cure. In practice these criteria are mingled together.

Analysis is likely to do harm. Because although one may

discover in the course of it various things about oneself, one must have a very strong and keen and persistent criticism in order to recognize and see through the mythology that is offered or imposed on one. There is an inducement to say, 'Yes, of course, it must be like that'. A powerful mythology.

LECTURES ON RELIGIOUS BELIEF

I

An Austrian general said to someone: "I shall think of you after my death, if that should be possible." We can imagine one group who would find this ludicrous, another who wouldn't.

(During the war, Wittgenstein saw consecrated bread being carried in chromium steel. This struck him as ludicrous.)

Suppose that someone believed in the Last Judgement, and I don't, does this mean that I believe the opposite to him, just that there won't be such a thing? I would say: "not at all, or not always."

Suppose I say that the body will rot, and another says "No. Particles will rejoin in a thousand years, and there will be a Resurrection of you."

If some said: "Wittgenstein, do you believe in this?" I'd say: "No." "Do you contradict the man?" I'd say: "No."

If you say this, the contradiction already lies in this.

Would you say: "I believe the opposite", or "There is no reason to suppose such a thing"? I'd say neither.

Suppose someone were a believer and said: "I believe in a Last Judgement," and I said: "Well, I'm not so sure. Possibly." You would say that there is an enormous gulf between us. If he said "There is a German aeroplane overhead," and I said "Possibly. I'm not so sure," you'd say we were fairly near.

It isn't a question of my being anywhere near him, but on an entirely different plane, which you could express by saying: "You mean something altogether different, Wittgenstein."

The difference might not show up at all in any explanation of the meaning.

Why is it that in this case I seem to be missing the entire point?

Suppose somebody made this guidance for this life: believing in the Last Judgment. Whenever he does anything, this is before his mind. In a way, how are we to know whether to say he believes this will happen or not?

Asking him is not enough. He will probably say he has proof.

But he has what you might call an unshakeable belief. It will show, not by reasoning or by appeal to ordinary grounds for belief, but rather by regulating for all in his life.

This is a very much stronger fact—foregoing pleasures, always appealing to this picture. This is one sense must be called the firmest of all beliefs, because the man risks things on account of it which he would not do on things which are by far better established for him. Although he distinguishes between things well-established and not well-established.

Lewy: Surely, he would say it is extremely well-established.

First, he may use "well-established" or not use it at all. He will treat this belief as extremely well-established, and in another way as not well-established at all.

If we have a belief, in certain cases we appeal again and again to certain grounds, and at the same time we risk pretty little—if it came to risking our lives on the ground of this belief.

There are instances where you have a faith—where you say "I believe"—and on the other hand this belief does not rest on the fact on which our ordinary everyday beliefs normally do rest.

How should we compare beliefs with each other? What would it mean to compare them?

You might say: 'We compare the states of mind."

How do we compare states of mind? This obviously won't do for all occasions. First, what you say won't be taken as the measure for the firmness of a belief? But, for instance, what risks you would take?

The strength of a belief is not comparable with the intensity of a pain.

An entirely different way of comparing beliefs is seeing what sorts of grounds he will give.

A belief isn't like a momentary state of mind. "At 5 o'clock he had very bad toothache."

Suppose you had two people, and one of them, when he had to decide which course to take, thought of retribution, and the other did not. One person might, for instance, be inclined to take everything that happened to him as a reward or punishment, and another person doesn't think of this at all.

If he is ill, he may think: "What have I done to deserve this?" This is one way of thinking of retribution. Another way is, he thinks in a general way whenever he is ashamed of himself: "This will be punished."

Take two people, one of whom talks of his behaviour and of what happens to him in terms of retribution, the other one does not. These people think entirely differently. Yet, so far, you can't say they believe different things.

Suppose someone is ill and he says: "This is a punishment," and I say: "If I'm ill, I don't think of punishment at all." If you say: "Do you believe the opposite?"—you can call it believing the opposite, but it is entirely different from what we would normally call believing the opposite.

I think differently, in a different way. I say different things to myself. I have different pictures.

It is this way: if someone said: "Wittgenstein, you don't take illness as punishment, so what do you believe?"—I'd say: "I don't have any thoughts of punishment."

There are, for instance, these entirely different ways of thinking first of all—which needn't be expressed by one person saying one thing, another person another thing.

What we call believing in a Judgement Day or not believing in a Judgement Day—The expression of belief may play an absolutely minor role.

If you ask me whether or not I believe in a Judgement Day, in the sense in which religious people have belief in it, I wouldn't say: "No. I don't believe there will be such a thing." It would seem to me utterly crazy to say this.

And then I give an explanation: "I don't believe in . . .", but then the religious person never believes what I describe.

I can't say. I can't contradict that person.

In one sense, I understand all he says—the English words "God", "separate", etc. I understand. I could say: "I don't believe in this," and this would be true, meaning I haven't got these thoughts or anything that hangs together with them. But not that I could contradict the thing.

You might say: "Well, if you can't contradict him, that means you don't understand him. If you did understand him, then you might." That again is Greek to me. My normal technique of language leaves me. I don't know whether to say they understand one another or not.

These controversies look quite different from any normal controversies. Reasons look entirely different from normal reasons.

They are, in a way, quite inconclusive.

The point is that if there were evidence, this would in fact destroy the whole business.

Anything that I normally call evidence wouldn't in the slightest influence me.

Suppose, for instance, we knew people who foresaw the future; make forecasts for years and years ahead; and they described some sort of a Judgement Day. Queerly enough, even if there were such a thing, and even if it were more convincing than I have described, belief in this happening wouldn't be at all a religious belief.

Suppose that I would have to forego all pleasures because of such a forecast. If I do so and so, someone will put me in fires in a thousand years, etc. I wouldn't budge. The best scientific evidence is just nothing.

A religious belief might in fact fly in the face of such a forecast, and say "No. There it will break down."

As it were, the belief as formulated on the evidence can only be the last result—in which a number of ways of thinking and acting crystallize and come together.

A man would fight for his life not to be dragged into the fire. No induction. Terror. That is, as it were, part of the substance of the belief.

That is partly why you don't get in religious controversies, the form of controversy where one person is *sure* of the thing, and the other says: 'Well, possibly.'

You might be surprised that there hasn't been opposed to those who believe in Resurrection those who say "Well, possibly."

Here believing obviously plays much more this role: suppose we said that a certain picture might play the role of constantly admonishing me, or I always think of it. Here, an enormous difference would be between those people for whom the picture is constantly in the foreground, and the others who just didn't use it at all.

Those who said: "Well, possibly it may happen and possibly not" would be on an entirely different plane.

This is partly why one would be reluctant to say: "These people rigorously hold the opinion (or view) that there is a Last Judgement". "Opinion" sounds queer.

It is for this reason that different words are used: 'dogma', 'faith'.

We don't talk about hypothesis, or about high probability. Nor about knowing.

In a religious discourse we use such expressions as: "I believe that so and so will happen," and use them differently to the way in which we use them in science.

Although, there is a great temptation to think we do. Because we do talk of evidence, and do talk of evidence by experience.

We could even talk of historic events.

It has been said that Christianity rests on an historic basis.

It has been said a thousand times by intelligent people that indubitability is not enough in this case. Even if there is as much evidence as for Napoleon. Because the indubitability wouldn't be enough to make me change my whole life.

It doesn't rest on an historic basis in the sense that the ordinary belief in historic facts could serve as a foundation.

Here we have a belief in historic facts different from a belief in ordinary historic facts. Even, they are not treated as historical, empirical, propositions.

Those people who had faith didn't apply the doubt which would ordinarily apply to *any* historical propositions. Especially propositions of a time long past, etc.

What is the criterion of reliability, dependability? Suppose you give a general description as to when you say a proposition has a reasonable weight of probability. When you call it reasonable, is this *only* to say that for it you have such and such evidence, and for others you haven't?

For instance, we don't trust the account given of an event by a drunk man.

Father O'Hara[1] is one of those people who make it a question of science.

Here we have people who treat this evidence in a different way. They base things on evidence which taken in one way would

[1] Contribution to a Symposium on *Science and Religion* (Lond: Gerald Howe, 1931, pp. 107–116).

E

seem exceedingly flimsy. They base enormous things on this evidence. Am I to say they are unreasonable? I wouldn't call them unreasonable.

I would say, they are certainly not *reasonable*, that's obvious.

'Unreasonable' implies, with everyone, rebuke.

I want to say: they don't treat this as a matter of reasonability.

Anyone who reads the Epistles will find it said: not only that it is not reasonable, but that it is folly.

Not only is it not reasonable, but it doesn't pretend to be.

What seems to me ludicrous about O'Hara is his making it appear to be *reasonable*.

Why shouldn't one form of life culminate in an utterance of belief in a Last Judgement? But I couldn't either say "Yes" or "No" to the statement that there will be such a thing. Nor "Perhaps," nor "I'm not sure."

It is a statement which may not allow of any such answer.

If Mr. Lewy is religious and says he believes in a Judgement Day, I won't even know whether to say I understand him or not. I've read the same things as he's read. In a most important sense, I know what he means.

If an atheist says: "There won't be a Judgment Day, and another person says there will," do they mean the same?—Not clear what criterion of meaning the same is. They might describe the same things. You might say, this already shows that they mean the same.

We come to an island and we find beliefs there, and certain beliefs we are inclined to call religious. What I'm driving at is, that religious beliefs will not . . . They have sentences, and there are also religious statements.

These statements would not just differ in respect to what they are about. Entirely different connections would make them into religious beliefs, and there can easily be imagined transitions where we wouldn't know for our life whether to call them religious beliefs or scientific beliefs.

You may say they reason wrongly.

In certain cases you would say they reason wrongly, meaning they contradict us. In other cases you would say they don't reason at all, or "It is an entirely different kind of reasoning." The first, you would say in the case in which they reason in a similar way to us, and make something corresponding to our blunders.

Whether a thing is a blunder or not—it is a blunder in a particular system. Just as something is a blunder in a particular game and not in another.

You could also say that where we are reasonable, they are not reasonable—meaning they don't use *reason* here.

If they do something very like one of our blunders, I would say, I don't know. It depends on further surroundings of it.

It is difficult to see, in cases in which it has all the appearances of trying to be reasonable.

I would definitely call O'Hara unreasonable. I would say, if this is religious belief, then it's all superstition.

But I would ridicule it, not by saying it is based on insufficient evidence. I would say: here is a man who is cheating himself. You can say: this man is ridiculous because he believes, and bases it on weak reasons.

II

The word 'God' is amongst the earliest learnt—pictures and catechisms, etc. But not the same consequences as with pictures of aunts. I wasn't shown [that which the picture pictured].

The word is used like a word representing a person. God sees, rewards, etc.

"Being shown all these things, did you understand what this word meant?" I'd say: "Yes and no. I did learn what it didn't mean. I made myself understand. I could answer questions, understand questions when they were put in different ways—and in that sense could be said to understand."

If the question arises as to the existence of a god or God, it plays an entirely different role to that of the existence of any person or object I ever heard of. One said, had to say, that one *believed* in the existence, and if one did not believe, this was regarded as something bad. Normally if I did not believe in the existence of something no one would think there was anything wrong in this.

Also, there is this extraordinary use of the word 'believe'. One talks of believing and at the same time one doesn't use 'believe' as one does ordinarily. You might say (in the normal

use): "You only believe—oh well. . . ." Here it is used entirely
differently; on the other hand it is not used as we generally use
the word 'know'.

If I even vaguely remember what I was taught about God, I
might say: "Whatever believing in God may be, it can't be believing in something we can test, or find means of testing." You
might say: "This is nonsense, because people say they believe on
evidence or say they believe on religious experiences." I would say:
"The mere fact that someone says they believe on evidence
doesn't tell me enough for me to be able to say now whether I
can say of a sentence 'God exists' that your evidence is unsatisfactory or insufficient."

Suppose I know someone, Smith. I've heard that he has been
killed in a battle in this war. One day you come to me and say:
"Smith is in Cambridge." I inquire, and find you stood at Guild-
hall and saw at the other end a man and said: "That was Smith."
I'd say: "Listen. This isn't sufficient evidence." If we had a fair
amount of evidence he was killed I would try to make you say
that you're being credulous. Suppose he was never heard of
again. Needless to say, it is quite impossible to make inquiries:
"Who at 12.05 passed Market Place into Rose Crescent?" Suppose
you say: "He was there". I would be extremely puzzled.

Suppose there is a feast on Mid-Summer Common. A lot of
people stand in a ring. Suppose this is done every year and then
everyone says he has seen one of his dead relatives on the other
side of the ring. In this case, we could ask everyone in the ring.
"Who did you hold by the hand?" Nevertheless, we'd all say that
on that day we see our dead relatives. You could in this case
say: "I had an extraordinary experience. I had the experience I
can express by saying: 'I saw my dead cousin'." Would we say
you are saying this on insufficient evidence? Under certain
circumstances I would say this, under other circumstances I
wouldn't. Where what is said sounds a bit absurd I would say:
"Yes, in this case insufficient evidence." If altogether absurd,
then I wouldn't.

Suppose I went to somewhere like Lourdes in France.
Suppose I went with a very credulous person. There we see blood
coming out of something. He says: "There you are, Wittgenstein,
how can you doubt?" I'd say: "Can it only be explained one way?

Can't it be this or that?" I'd try to convince him that he'd seen nothing of any consequence. I wonder whether I would do that under all circumstances. I certainly know that I would under normal circumstances.

"Oughtn't one after all to consider this?" I'd say: "Come on. Come on." I would treat the phenomenon in this case just as I would treat an experiment in a laboratory which I thought badly executed.

"The balance moves when I will it to move." I point out it is not covered up, a draught can move it, etc.

I could imagine that someone showed an extremely passionate belief in such a phenomenon, and I couldn't approach his belief at all by saying: "This could just as well have been brought about by so and so" because he could think this blasphemy on my side. Or he might say: "It is possible that these priests cheat, but nevertheless in a different sense a miraculous phenomenon takes place there."

I have a statue which bleeds on such and such a day in the year. I have red ink, etc. "You are a cheat, but nevertheless the Deity uses you. Red ink in a sense, but not red ink in a sense."

Cf. Flowers at seance with label. People said: "Yes, flowers are materialized with label." What kind of circumstances must there be to make this kind of story not ridiculous?

I have a moderate education, as all of you have, and therefore know what is meant by insufficient evidence for a forecast. Suppose someone dreamt of the Last Judgement, and said he now knew what it would be like. Suppose someone said: "This is poor evidence." I would say: "If you want to compare it with the evidence for it's raining to-morrow it is no evidence at all." He may make it sound as if by stretching the point you may call it evidence. But it may be more than ridiculous as evidence. But now, would I be prepared to say: "You are basing your belief on extremely slender evidence, to put it mildly." Why should I regard this dream as evidence—measuring its validity as though I were measuring the validity of the evidence for meteorological events?

If you compare it with anything in Science which we call evidence, you can't credit that anyone could soberly argue: "Well, I had this dream . . . therefore . . . Last Judgement". You might say: "For a blunder, that's too big." If you suddenly wrote numbers down on the blackboard, and then said: "Now, I'm going to add," and then said: "2 and 21 is 13," etc. I'd say: "This is no blunder."

There are cases where I'd say he's mad, or he's making fun. Then there might be cases where I look for an entirely different interpretation altogether. In order to see what the explanation is I should have to see the sum, to see in what way it is done, what he makes follow from it, what are the different circumstances under which he does it, etc.

I mean, if a man said to me after a dream that he believed in the Last Judgement, I'd try to find what sort of impression it gave him. One attitude: "It will be in about 2,000 years. It will be bad for so and so and so, etc." Or it may be one of terror. In the case where there is hope, terror, etc., would I say there is insufficient evidence if he says: "I believe . . ."? I can't treat these words as I normally treat 'I believe so and so'. It would be entirely beside the point, and also if he said his friend so and so and his grandfather had had the dream and believed, it would be entirely beside the point.

I would not say: "If a man said he dreamt it would happen to-morrow, would he take his coat?", etc.

Case where Lewy has visions of his dead friend. Cases where you don't try to locate him. And case where you try to locate him in a business-like way. Another case where I'd say: "We can presuppose we have a broad basis on which we agree."

In general, if you say: "He is dead" and I say: "He is not dead" no one would say: "Do they mean the same thing by 'dead'?" In the case where a man has visions I wouldn't offhand say: "He means something different."

Cf.   A person having persecution mania.

What is the criterion for meaning something different? Not only what he takes as evidence for it, but also how he reacts, that he is in terror, etc.

How am I to find out whether this proposition is to be regarded as an empirical proposition—'You'll see your dead friend again?' Would I say: "He is a bit superstitious?" Not a bit.

He might have been apologetic. (The man who stated it

categorically was more intelligent than the man who was apologetic about it).

'Seeing a dead friend,' again means nothing much to me at all. I don't think in these terms. I don't say to myself: "I shall see so and so again" ever.

He always says it, but he doesn't make any search. He puts on a queer smile. "His story had that dreamlike quality." My answer would be in this case "Yes," and a particular explanation.

Take "God created man". Pictures of Michelangelo showing the creation of the world. In general, there is nothing which explains the meanings of words as well as a picture, and I take it that Michelangelo was as good as anyone can be and did his best, and here is the picture of the Deity creating Adam.

If we ever saw this, we certainly wouldn't think this the Deity. The picture has to be used in an entirely different way if we are to call the man in that queer blanket 'God', and so on. You could imagine that religion was taught by means of these pictures. "Of course, we can only express ourselves by means of picture." This is rather queer . . . I could show Moore the pictures of a tropical plant. There is a technique of comparison between picture and plant. If I showed him the picture of Michelangelo and said: "Of course, I can't show you the real thing, only the picture" . . . . The absurdity is, I've never taught him the technique of using this picture.

It is quite clear that the role of pictures of Biblical subjects and role of the picture of God creating Adam are totally different ones. You might ask this question: "Did Michelangelo think that Noah in the ark looked like this, and that God creating Adam looked like this?" He wouldn't have said that God or Adam looked as they look in this picture.

It might seem as though, if we asked such a question as: "Does Lewy *really* mean what so and so means when he says so and so is alive?"—it might seem as though there were two sharply divided cases, one in which he would say he didn't mean it literally. I want to say this is not so. There will be cases where we will differ, and where it won't be a question at all of more or less knowledge, so that we can come together. Sometimes it will be a question of experience, so you can say: "Wait another 10 years." And I would say: "I would disencourage this kind of

reasoning" and Moore would say: "I wouldn't disencourage it."
That is, one would *do* something. We would take sides, and that
goes so far that there would really be great differences between
us, which might come out in Mr. Lewy saying: "Wittgenstein is
trying to undermine reason", and this wouldn't be false. This is
actually where such questions rise.

III

Today I saw a poster saying: " 'Dead' Undergraduate speaks."

The inverted commas mean: "He isn't really dead." "He isn't what people call dead. They call it 'dead' not quite correctly."

We don't speak of "door" in quotes.

It suddenly struck me: "If someone said 'He isn't really dead, although by the ordinary criteria he is dead'—couldn't I say "He is not only dead by the ordinary criteria; he is what we all call 'dead'."

If you now call him 'alive', you're using language in a queer way, because you're almost deliberately preparing misunderstandings. Why don't you use some other word, and let "dead" have the meaning it already has?

Suppose someone said: "It didn't always have this meaning. He's not dead according to the old meaning" or "He's not dead according to the old idea".

What is it, to have different ideas of death? Suppose you say: "I have the idea of myself being a chair after death" or "I have the idea of myself being a chair in half-an-hour"—you all know under what circumstances we say of something that it has become a chair.

Cf. (1) "This shadow will cease to exist."

(2) "This chair will cease to exist." You say that you know what this chair ceasing to exist is like. But you have to think. You may find that there isn't a use for this sentence. You think of the use.

I imagine myself on the death-bed. I imagine you all looking at the air above me. You say "You have an idea".

Are you clear when you'd say you had ceased to exist?

You have six different ideas [of 'ceasing to exist'] at different times.

If you say: "I can imagine myself being a disembodied spirit. Wittgenstein, can you imagine yourself as a disembodied spirit?" —I'd say: "I'm sorry. I [so far] connect nothing with these words."

I connect all sorts of complicated things with these words. I think of what people have said of sufferings after death, etc.

"I have two different ideas, one of ceasing to exist after death, the other of being a disembodied spirit."

What's it like to have two different ideas? What is the criterion for one man having one idea, another man having another idea?

You gave me two phrases, "ceasing to exist", "being a disembodied spirit". "When I say this, I think of myself having a certain set of experiences." What is it like to think of this?

If you think of your brother in America, how do you know that what you think is, that the thought inside you is, of your brother being in America? Is this an experiential business?

Cf. How do you know that what you want is an apple? [Russell].

How do you know that you believe that your brother is in America?

A pear might be what satisfied you. But you wouldn't say: "What I wanted was an apple."

Suppose we say that the thought is some sort of process in his mind, or his saying something, etc.—then I could say: "All right, you call this a thought of your brother in America, well, what is the connection between this and your brother in America?"

Lewy: You might say that this is a question of convention.

Why is it that you don't doubt that it is a thought of your brother in America?

One process [the thought] seems to be a shadow or a picture of something else.

How do I know that a picture is a picture of Lewy?—Normally by its likeness to Lewy, or, under certain circumstances, a picture of Lewy may not be like him, but like Smith. If I give up the business of being like [as a criterion], I get into an awful mess, because anything may be his portrait, given a certain method of projection.

If you said that the thought was in some way a picture of his brother in America—Yes, but by what method of projection is it a picture of this? How queer it is that there should be no doubt what it's a picture of.

If you're asked: "How do you know it is a thought of such and such?" the thought that immediately comes to your mind is one of a shadow, a picture. You don't think of a causal relation. The kind of relation you think of is best expressed by "picture", "shadow," etc.

The word "picture" is even quite all right—in many cases it is even in the most ordinary sense, a picture. You might translate my very words into a picture.

But the point is this, suppose you drew this, how do I know it is my brother in America? Who says it is him—unless it is here ordinary similarity?

What is the connection between these words, or anything substitutable for them, with my brother in America?

The first idea [you have] is that you are looking at your own thought, and are absolutely sure that it is a thought that so and so. You are looking at some mental phenomenon, and you say to yourself "obviously this is a thought of my brother being in America". It seems to be a super-picture. It seems, with thought, that there is no doubt whatever. With a picture, it still depends on the method of projection, whereas here it seems that you get rid of the projecting relation, and are absolutely certain that this is thought of that.

Smythies's muddle is based on the idea of a super-picture.

We once talked about how the idea of certain superlatives came about in Logic. The idea of a super-necessity, etc.

"How do I know that this is the thought of my brother in America?"—that *what* is the thought?

Suppose my thought consists of my *saying* "My brother is in America"—how do I know that I *say* my brother is in America?

How is the connection made?—We imagine at first a connection like strings.

Lewy: The connection is a convention. The word designates.

You must explain "designates" by examples. We have learnt a rule, a practice, etc.

Is thinking of something like painting or shooting at something?

It seems like a projection connection, which seems to make it indubitable, although there is not a projection relation at all.

If I said "My brother is in America"—I could imagine there being rays projecting from my words to my brother in America. But what if my brother isn't in America?—then the rays don't hit anything.

[If you say that the words refer to my brother by expressing the proposition that my brother is in America—the proposition

being a middle link between the words and what they refer to]
—What has the proposition, the mediate link, got to do with
America?

The most important point is this—if you talk of painting, etc.
your idea is that the connection exists *now*, so that it seems as
though as long as I do this thinking, this connection exists.

Whereas, if we said it is a connection of convention, there
would be no point in saying it exists while we think. There is a
connection by convention—What do we mean?—This connection
refers to events happening at various times. Most of all, it refers
to a technique.

["Is thinking something going on at a particular time, or is it
spread over the words?" "It comes in a flash." "Always?—it
sometimes does come in a flash, although this may be all sorts of
different things."]

If it does refer to a technique, then it can't be enough, in
certain cases, to explain what you mean in a few words; because
there is something which might be thought to be in conflict with
the idea going on from 7 to 7.5, namely the practice of using it
[the phrase.]

When we talked of: "So and so is an automaton", the strong
hold of that view was [due to the idea] that you could say: "Well,
I know what I mean" . . . , as though you were looking at something happening while you said the thing, entirely independent of
what came before and after, the application [of the phrase]. It
looked as though you could talk of understanding a word,
without any reference to the technique of its usage. It looked as
though Smythies said he could understand the sentence, and that
we then had nothing to say.

What was it like to have different ideas of death?—What I
meant was—Is having an idea of death something like having a
certain picture, so that you can say "I have an idea of death from
5 to 5.1 etc."? "In whatever way anyone will use this word, I
have now a certain idea"—if you call this "having an idea", then
it is not what is commonly called "having an idea", because
what is commonly called "having an idea", has a reference to the
technique of the word, etc.

We are all here using the word "death", which is a public

instrument, which has a whole technique [of usage]. Then someone says he has an idea of death. Something queer; because you might say "You are using the word 'death', which is an instrument functioning in a certain way."

If you treat this [your idea] as something private, with what right are you calling it an idea of death?—I say this, because we, also, have a right to say what is an idea of death.

He might say "I have my own private idea of death"—why call this an 'idea of death' unless it is something you connect with death. Although this [your 'idea'] might not interest us at all. [In this case,] it does not belong on the game played with 'death', which we all know and understand.

If what he calls his "idea of death" is to become relevant, it must become part of our game.

'My idea of death is the separation of the soul from the body' —if we know what to do with these words. He can also say: "I connect with the word 'death' a certain picture—a woman lying in her bed"—that may or may not be of some interest.

If he connects

with death, and this was his idea, this might be interesting psychologically.

"The separation of soul from body" [only had a public interest.] This may act like black curtains or it may not act like black curtains. I'd have to find out what the consequences [of your saying it] are. I am not, at least, at present at all clear. [You say this]—"So what?"—I know these words, I have certain pictures. All sorts of things go along with these words.

If he says this, I won't know yet what consequences he will draw. I don't know what he opposes this to.

Lewy: You oppose it to being extinguished.

If you say to me—"Do you cease to exist?"—I should be bewildered, and would not know what exactly this is to mean.

"If you don't cease to exist, you will suffer after death", there I begin to attach ideas, perhaps ethical ideas of responsibility. The point is, that although these are well-known words, and although I can go from one sentence to another sentence, or to pictures [I don't know what consequences you draw from this statement].

Suppose someone said: "What do you believe, Wittgenstein? Are you a sceptic? Do you know whether you will survive death?" I would really, this is a fact, say "I can't say. I don't know", because I haven't any clear idea what I'm saying when I'm saying "I don't cease to exist," etc.

Spiritualists make one kind of connection.

A Spiritualist says "Apparition" etc. Although he gives me a picture I don't like, I do get a clear idea. I know that much, that some people connect this phrase with a particular kind of verification. I know that some people don't—religious people e.g.—they don't refer to a verification, but have entirely different ideas.

A great writer said that, when he was a boy, his father set him a task, and he suddenly felt that nothing, not even death, could take away the responsibility [in doing this task]; this was his duty to do, and that even death couldn't stop it being his duty. He said that this was, in a way, a proof of the immortality of the soul—because if this lives on [the responsibility won't die.] The idea is given by what we call the proof. Well, if this is the idea, [all right].

If a Spiritualist wishes to give *me* an idea of what he means or doesn't mean by 'survival', he can say all sorts of things—

[If I ask what idea he has, I may be given what the Spiritualists say or I may be given what the man I quoted said, etc., etc.]

I would at least [in the case of the Spiritualist] have an idea of what this sentence is connected up with, and get more and more of an idea as I see what he does with it.

As it is, I hardly connect anything with it at all.

Suppose someone, before going to China, when he might never see me again, said to me: "We might see one another after death"—would I necessarily say that I don't understand him? I might say [want to say] simply, "Yes. I *understand* him entirely."

Lewy: In this case, you might only mean that he expressed a certain attitude.

I would say "No, it isn't the same as saying 'I'm very fond of you' "—and it may not be the same as saying anything else. It says what it says. Why should you be able to substitute anything else?

Suppose I say: "The man used a picture."

"Perhaps now he sees he was wrong." What sort of remark is this?

"God's eye sees everything"—I want to say of this that it uses a picture.

I don't want to belittle him [the person who says it.]

Suppose I said to him "You've been using a picture", and he said "No, this is not all"—mightn't he have misunderstood me? What do I want to do [by saying this]? What would be the real sign of disagreement? What might be the real criterion of his disagreeing with me?

Lewy: If he said: 'I've been making preparations [for death].'

Yes, this might be a disagreement—if he himself were to use the word in a way in which I did not expect, or were to draw conclusions I did not expect him to draw. I wanted only to draw attention to a particular technique of usage. We should disagree, if he was using a technique I didn't expect.

We associate a particular use with a picture.

Smythies: This isn't all he does—associate a use with a picture.

Wittgenstein: Rubbish. I meant: what conclusions are you going to draw? etc. Are eyebrows going to be talked of, in connection with the Eye of God?

"He could just as well have said so and so"—this [remark] is foreshadowed by the word "attitude". He couldn't just as well have said something else.

If I say he used a picture, I don't want to say anything he himself wouldn't say. I want to say that he draws these conclusions.

Isn't it as important as anything else, what picture he does use?

Of certain pictures we say that they might just as well be replaced by another—e.g. we could, under certain circumstances, have one projection of an ellipse drawn instead of another.

[He *may* say]: "I would have been prepared to use another picture, it would have had the same effect. . . ."

The whole *weight* may be in the picture.

We can say in chess that the exact shape of the chess-men plays no role. Suppose that the main pleasure was, to see people ride; then, playing it in writing wouldn't be playing the same game. Someone might say: "All he's done is change the shape of the head"—what more could he do?

When I say he's using a picture I'm merely making a *grammatical* remark: [What I say] can only be verified by the consequences he does or does not draw.

If Smythies disagrees, I don't take notice of this disagreement.

All I wished to characterize was the conventions he wished to draw. If I wished to say anything more I was merely being philosophically arrogant.

Normally, if you say "He is an automaton " you draw consequences, if you stab him, [he'll not feel pain]. On the other hand, you may not wish to draw any such consequences, and this is all there is to it—except further muddles.